The Resurrection Power of God

The Resurrection Power of God

© 2016 by Bill Vincent.

PUBLISHED BY REVIVAL WAVES OF GLORY
BOOKS & PUBLISHING

www.revivalwavesofgloryministries.com

Litchfield, IL

The Resurrection Power of God
(Second Edition)

Great Exploits of God

By Bill Vincent

The Resurrection Power of God

Table of Content

Holy Ghost Power

There is fresh baptism of the Holy Ghost coming. I want to bring the true meaning of what it means to be baptized or filled with the Holy Spirit. Most people would say I already have been filled with the Spirit and speak in tongues.

I want to talk about the Baptisms (Plural) of the Holy Spirit.

Matthew 3:11 I indeed baptize you with water unto repentance: but he that cometh after me is mightier than I, whose shoes I am not worthy to bear: he shall baptize you with the Holy Ghost, and *with* fire:

More than once Jesus referred to a baptism of the Holy Spirit and fire.

6

Is there more than one kind of baptism from God? The disciples were filled and were filled again. Paul talked about being filled and keep on being filled. There is more than just one simple filling of the Holy Spirit. I want to talk about 3 different baptisms of fire. Heb. 6: would be a good study about many baptisms. (The doctrine of baptisms.)

We as a Church have lost something concerning the Baptisms of the Holy Ghost. There are more than just speaking in tongues. The baptism of the Holy Spirit has become a form.... A FORM of Godliness but denying the power there of.

We have accepted signs of the baptism "speaking in tongues" as the fullness of what God intended. We have settled for less. We have a form of being filled with the Holy Spirit. The Church is not turning the world up side down.

John G. Lake walked in miracles for eight years before he ever spoke in tongues. There is power in being filled. Smith Wigglesworth had many years of miracles and then when he was going to be filled with the Spirit he fasted and prayed for ten days to get ready to be filled. True Baptism of the Holy Spirit doesn't come easy, esp. if you are talking about resurrection power. I'm going to talk about the baptism of power and the baptism of fire and how to receive it.

The first baptism of fire,

Mal. Chapter 3 Talks about the refiner's fire. So the first baptism of fire is, The Baptism of Holiness. There is a fire that comes to purge and then the Glory comes.

The Second baptism of fire,
Song of Solomon 8 talks about a consuming fire. This fire is different from the refiner's fire.

Song of Solomon 8:6 Set me as a seal upon thine heart, as a seal upon thine arm: for love *is* strong as death; jealousy *is* cruel as the grave: the coals thereof *are* coals of fire, *which hath a* most vehement flame.

The Second baptism (as above) of fire is the Baptism of intimacy or love of Jesus.

The third baptism is referred to the burning and shining lamp.

It's the Acts Chapter 2 of be my witness be my flame.

The third baptism (as above) of fire is,

the Baptism of fiery witness.

You cannot have the baptism of power without fire of holiness, fire intimacy, and a fiery witness.

Luke 24:49 And, behold, I send the promise of my Father upon you: but tarry ye in the city of Jerusalem, until ye be endued with power from on high.

Holy desperation is where we find power.

John 20:20 And when he had so said, he shewed unto them *his* hands and his side. Then were the disciples glad, when they saw the Lord.

Acts 2:4 And they were all filled with the Holy Ghost, and began to speak with other tongues, as the Spirit gave them utterance.

(Filled again)

How can a person be really filled with the fullness of God's Spirit without signs, wonders, healings, miracles, and resurrection of the dead?

Acts 1:5 For John truly baptized with water; but ye shall be baptized with the Holy Ghost not many days hence.

Why days?

Prophetic Word: We are re-digging old wells like Azusa Street Revival.

Acts 1:8 But ye shall receive power, after that the Holy Ghost is come upon you: and ye shall be witnesses unto me both in Jerusalem, and in all Judaea, and in Samaria, and unto the uttermost part of the earth.

That is an experience. Some of the faith movements have suggested that encounters and experiencing the God of the Universe is just by faith instead of a real experience. We are to speak in new tongues but there is so much more through baptisms of fire.

Please read this next passage of scripture and compare it to our day.

Acts 19:1-41 And it came to pass, that, while Apollos was at Corinth, Paul having passed through the upper coasts came to Ephesus: and finding certain disciples, He said unto them, Have ye received the Holy Ghost since ye believed? And they said unto him, We have not so much as heard whether there be any Holy Ghost. And he said unto them, Unto what then were ye baptized? And they said, Unto John's baptism. Then said Paul, John verily baptized with the baptism of repentance, saying unto the people, that they should believe on him which should come after him, that is, on Christ Jesus. When they heard *this,* they were baptized in the name of the Lord Jesus. And when Paul had laid *his* hands upon them, the Holy Ghost came on them; and they spake with tongues, and prophesied. And all the men were about twelve. And he went into the synagogue, and spake boldly for the space of three months, disputing and persuading the things concerning the kingdom of God. And this continued by the space of two years; so that all they which dwelt in Asia heard the word of the Lord Jesus, both Jews and Greeks. And God wrought special miracles by the hands of Paul: So that from his body were brought unto the sick handkerchiefs or aprons, and the diseases departed from them, and the evil spirits went out of them. Then certain of the vagabond Jews, exorcists, took upon them to call over them which had evil spirits the name of the Lord

Jesus, saying, We adjure you by Jesus whom Paul preacheth. And there were seven sons of *one* Sceva, a Jew, *and* chief of the priests, which did so. And the evil spirit answered and said, Jesus I know, and Paul I know; but who are ye? And the man in whom the evil spirit was leaped on them, and overcame them, and prevailed against them, so that they fled out of that house naked and wounded. And this was known to all the Jews and Greeks also dwelling at Ephesus; and fear fell on them all, and the name of the Lord Jesus was magnified. And many that believed came, and confessed, and shewed their deeds. Many of them also which used curious arts brought their books together, and burned them before all *men:* and they counted the price of them, and found *it* fifty thousand *pieces* of silver. So mightily grew the word of God and prevailed. After these things were ended, Paul purposed in the spirit, when he had passed through Macedonia and Achaia, to go to Jerusalem, saying, After I have been there, I must also see Rome. So he sent into Macedonia two of them that ministered unto him, Timotheus and Erastus; but he himself stayed in Asia for a season. And the same time there arose no small stir about that way. For a certain *man* named Demetrius, a silversmith, which made silver shrines for Diana, brought no small gain unto the craftsmen; Whom he called together with the workmen of like occupation, and said, Sirs, ye know that by this craft we have our wealth. Moreover ye see and hear, that not alone at Ephesus, but almost throughout all Asia, this Paul hath persuaded and turned away much people, saying that they be no gods, which are made with hands: So that not only this our craft is in danger to be set at nought; but also that the temple of the great goddess Diana should be despised, and her magnificence should be destroyed, whom all Asia and the world worshippeth. And when they heard *these sayings,* they were full of wrath, and cried out, saying, Great *is* Diana of the Ephesians. And the whole city was filled with confusion: and having caught Gaius and Aristarchus, men of Macedonia, Paul's companions in travel, they rushed with one accord into the theatre. And when Paul would have entered in unto the people, the disciples suffered him not. And certain of the chief of Asia, which were his friends, sent unto him, desiring *him* that he would not adventure himself into the theatre. Some therefore cried one thing, and some another: for the assembly was confused; and the more part knew not wherefore they were come together. And they drew Alexander out of the multitude, the Jews putting him forward. And Alexander beckoned with the hand, and would have made his defence unto the people. But when they knew that he was a Jew, all with one voice about the space of two hours cried out, Great *is* Diana of the Ephesians. And when the townclerk had appeased the people, he said, *Ye* men of Ephesus, what man is there that knoweth not how that the city of the Ephesians is a worshipper of the great goddess Diana, and of the

image which fell down from Jupiter?
Seeing then that these things
cannot be spoken against, ye ought
to be quiet, and to do nothing
rashly. For ye have brought hither
these men, which are neither
robbers of churches, nor yet
blasphemers of your goddess.
Wherefore if Demetrius, and the
craftsmen which are with him, have
a matter against any man, the law
is open, and there are deputies: let
them implead one another. But if ye
enquire any thing concerning other
matters, it shall be determined in a
lawful assembly. For we are in
danger to be called in question for
this day's uproar, there being no
cause whereby we may give an
account of this concourse. And
when he had thus spoken, he
dismissed the assembly.

Godly Inheritance

There is an inheritance coming to God's children. This is a Chapter where we will define what divine inheritances are. Also we'll take a look at what mantles are. Then we'll discuss how we come into divine inheritances and how divine inheritances affect the generations to come. We will also look at raising up the foundations of many generations and examining legal rights to a family's divine inheritance. Also we will discover which particular mantle is so essential and why this is so.

DIVINE INHERITANCES EXIST IN THE SPIRIT REALM

We often think of an inheritance as something physical such as a family heirloom, a sum of money or a piece of real estate that passes from one generation to the next when the benefactor dies. But there are spiritual inheritances as well as physical ones. We know that there is an inheritance in Christ because believers are joint heirs and we've been blessed with every spiritual blessing in the heavenly places in Christ.

Romans 8:17 And if children, then heirs; heirs of God, and joint-heirs with Christ; if so be that we suffer with *him,* that we may be also glorified together.

Ephesians 1:3 Blessed *be* the God and Father of our Lord Jesus Christ, who hath blessed us with all spiritual blessings in heavenly *places* in Christ:

In fact, this is the most important inheritance. But did you know that there are other inheritances, in fact, many inheritances that exist and are available to us in the spirit realm?

God is speaking about inheritances, divine inheritances, and He wants to release them to us! Specifically, I saw that today we are going to receive, as a church, a revelation about divine inheritances and that we will learn how to steward what God gives us for our children's children.

Psalms 139:16 Thine eyes did see my substance, yet being unperfect; and in thy book all *my members* were written, *which* in continuance were fashioned, when *as yet there was* none of them.

God has ordained destiny for every human being before they are born. He has a plan, a purpose, a future and a hope for each of us. He has good works for us to accomplish. With this in mind I began to seek the Lord and I asked Him several questions, such as:

So what happens when children die and never receive their inheritance? What happens to the inheritance that God ordained for them? What about an aborted baby? What happens to that child's inheritance?

What happens to the ones like Jack Coe, at 36 years of age in the prime of his ministry, who died? Did anyone ever receive the mantle of Jack Coe, and what about his inheritance?

What about the people that never reach the fullness of what God ordained for them or who never came to know Jesus Christ as their personal Lord and Savior? Did God have a future and a hope for them? Does their inheritance become available in the spirit realm?

What happens in the spirit when people don't receive their inheritance? What happens to their inheritance in heaven?

The Lord responded to my questions with His question! "Their inheritances are available to you. Do you want them?" I thought, well how many can I have? He said, "Well, if they had been born and if they had received Jesus, I would have given them a great university or I would have given them two continents, or I would have given them an international deliverance ministry. You can have that because their destiny is still available in the spirit realm."

So I have come to understand that we can receive many inheritances. With this revelation vividly impressed upon me, I'm collecting inheritances! Do you know what divine inheritance means? Acquiring somebody else's testimony their story becomes your story. What they saw God do through their life becomes a reality for you. When I think about collecting inheritances I'm talking about believers collecting the testimonies of the works of the Lord in the lives of men and women over the last 2,000 years!

MANTLES

When we receive a mantle we're receiving from God, an authority, a power, a gift and a call. Scripture tell us that Elisha, the prophet, had a "double portion" of the spirit of Elijah, which is in fact, the mantle of Elijah.

2 Kings 2:9-14 And it came to pass, when they were gone over, that Elijah said unto Elisha, Ask what I shall do for thee, before I be taken away from thee. And Elisha said, I pray thee, let a double portion of thy spirit be upon me. And he said, Thou hast asked a hard thing: *nevertheless,* if thou see

me *when I am* taken from thee, it shall be so unto thee; but if not, it shall not be *so.* And it came to pass, as they still went on, and talked, that, behold, *there appeared* a chariot of fire, and horses of fire, and parted them both asunder; and Elijah went up by a whirlwind into heaven. And Elisha saw *it,* and he cried, My father, my father, the chariot of Israel, and the horsemen thereof. And he saw him no more: and he took hold of his own clothes, and rent them in two pieces. He took up also the mantle of Elijah that fell from him, and went back, and stood by the bank of Jordan; And he took the mantle of Elijah that fell from him, and smote the waters, and said, Where *is* the LORD God of Elijah? and when he also had smitten the waters, they parted hither and thither: and Elisha went over. Even Elisha didn't have many mantles. He had one double portion of the mantle of Elijah. As I said earlier, God is revealing that we can receive many inheritances but we usually do not receive more than one mantle.

I want to ask us two questions. The first is when are mantles available?

Let's take a look at 2 Kings 2:8-14. We see that Elisha asked (v. 9). This is a key. He asked for a hard thing, a double portion of the spirit of Elijah, the mantle of Elijah (vs. 9-10). After Elijah died, in the passing of Elijah into heaven, his mantle became available. So, in the passing of one generation, the time comes when a mantle becomes available. We can be like Elisha and ask for someone's mantle, even if it appears to be a "hard thing."

Now here's my second question. Where can mantles be found? We see with Elijah and Elisha that Elisha found Elijah's mantle because he would not leave Elijah's side (vs. 2, 4, and 6). Elisha persevered and stuck like glue to Elijah! The principle we need to see here is that mantles are found and then received when God sees that we earnestly desire His highest will, His highest plan for our lives. In other words, we're sticking like "crazy glue" to the Lord!

Also, where was the mantle of Elisha? It was where Elisha was buried! The mantle, that double portion, went to the grave with him.

Get this! Scripture tells us that when a dead man was thrown into the grave of Elisha that when his dead body touched the bones of Elisha the anointing that was on his bones caused the dead man to come to life! Why? It happened because he touched the mantle of Elisha which was the double portion of the spirit of Elijah, residing upon Elisha's bones. Wow!

It's interesting to note that when Elisha died, no one asked for his mantle! I'd like you to keep this in mind as I share a vision with you. A young man told this to me over seven years ago. He was taken in a vision into a valley where he saw mantles, like the garment of Elisha in 2 Kings 2:8, of Smith Wigglesworth, Kathryn Kuhlman, Martin Luther, Moses, Abraham and others. He saw the mantles that were upon the lives of great men and women who were used by God throughout history. He saw numbers of mantles, further than his eyes could see. Many mantles were torn and some were barely even used, as if the owners had never even put them on!

Other mantles were barely even tarnished or torn. The impact of this vision has remained with me to this day.

There are times in the spirit when our mantle can get torn and tarnished. And there are times in the spirit when our garment doesn't fit anymore and by that I mean there is room for another mantle upon our life. We can ask for a mantle like Elisha did (2 Kings 2:9) and God will give it if it's His will. As a matter of fact, Elijah invited Elisha to ask (v.9). However, there are times when we're not asking for a particular mantle and God will offer one of His choosing, to us. I believe the offer comes when God sees that we desire Him passionately, above all else.

In my life, the first mantle the Lord placed upon my life was an evangelist's mantle. I put that on and I was faithful with it and I grew into my mantle. About two years later God came along and He had a new mantle for me to wear. He said, "Do you like this one?" I said, "Yes, I like that. What is it Lord?" He said, "It's a prophet's mantle." I remember when I tried it on it didn't fit right at first.

I wasn't quite comfortable with my new identity because I was an evangelist and my identity was in the evangelistic mantle. But God said, "I want you to try this one on." Sometimes when we wear something new we wonder if it fits right. We can feel a little awkward in a new suit like we're "sticking out." "Wow!

I had to get comfortable with the prophet mantle and now it fits really well, like a glove. And then God came along and He said, "Bill, I have a new mantle for you! Look at this one!" It was called the apostolic mantle. When I saw it I said, "God, I don't want that one! I'll wear my evangelist's mantle; I'll wear my prophet's mantle but please don't put that "apostle-jacket" on me. It doesn't look right and it doesn't feel right! I was just getting comfortable in the prophet's mantle!"

It didn't take me long to surrender to the Lord and receive the apostolic mantle. I'm still growing into it. We grow into these things. The mantles will grow up with you! Remember when God brought the children of Israel out of Egypt? They were 40 years in the wilderness and they wore the same clothes and the same shoes for those 40 years. As they grew up their clothes and shoes grew with them! So we're growing into our mantle. There are three mantles that God placed on my life and I can't say that they represent the mantle of Martin Luther or John G. Lake or anyone else because each one is my mantle. I believe that it's time for believers to put on a new mantle. God is going to place a new mantle upon many believers reading this teaching and He's going to give us a revelation about divine inheritances, too!

INHERITING THE DESOLATE INHERITANCES

What did our forefathers leave us as an inheritance? On the surface, it looks like the answer is "nothing" because we really only have a faint memory about some of the revivals that went on 200 years ago. Also, how many ministries have fathered sons and daughters to continue their mandate and then pass it along as an inheritance to the next generation?

There are some great evangelists who have a legacy, but do they have sons and daughters who have inherited the work of the ministry and then carried it through and passed it on to the next generation as an inheritance? I believe the Lord is going to release an anointing on certain believers for bringing restoration that will cause men and women to come into inheritances that have been lost for many generations.

Isaiah 49:8 Thus saith the LORD, In an acceptable time have I heard thee, and in a day of salvation have I helped thee: and I will preserve thee, and give thee for a covenant of the people, to establish the earth, to cause to inherit the desolate heritages;

Have you ever thought about inheriting the inheritances that have become desolate? The meaning is: lost inheritances. The Lord said, "Bill I'm going to cause men and women to receive desolate heritages." The word heritage means inheritances.

Isaiah 58:12 And *they that shall be* of thee shall build the old waste places: thou shalt raise up the foundations of many generations; and thou shalt be called, The repairer of the breach, The restorer of paths to dwell in.

A key phrase from this scripture is: foundations of many generations. Could there be a generation today that God entrusts with the foundations of generations in the past because those generations lost what God gave them? Can we rebuild that? Is it possible that we can come into the very inheritance that God was entrusting to past generations and that we can rebuild it today and possess it in our lifetime? I believe the answer is "Yes!" We could raise up the foundations of many generations! Great, great potential! Think about that!

The prophet Isaiah says in the above scripture that "you will be called the 'Repairer of the Breech' and 'The Restorer of Streets to Dwell In.'" This means that there will be those who have an anointing for restoration and they will cause people to be restored to their path of destiny.

Some of you who have gotten off track are saying, "God, please give me a prophetic sense of who I am and where I am going. What is my identity and my purpose, what is my future and my hope?

Isaiah 61:1 The Spirit of the Lord GOD *is* upon me; because the LORD hath anointed me to preach good tidings unto the meek; he hath sent me to bind up the brokenhearted, to proclaim liberty to the captives, and the opening of the prison to *them that are* bound;

Luke 4:14-21 And Jesus returned in the power of the Spirit into Galilee: and there went out a fame of him through all the region round about. And he taught in their synagogues, being glorified of all. And he came to Nazareth, where he had been brought up: and, as his custom was, he went into the synagogue on the sabbath day, and stood up for to read. And there was delivered unto him the book of the prophet Esaias. And when he had opened the book, he found the place where it was written, The Spirit of the Lord *is* upon me, because he hath anointed me to preach the gospel to the poor; he hath sent me to heal the brokenhearted, to preach deliverance to the captives, and recovering of sight to the blind, to set at liberty them that are bruised, To preach the acceptable year of the Lord. And he closed the book, and he gave *it* again to the minister, and sat down. And the eyes of all them that were in the synagogue were fastened on him. And he began to say unto them, This day is this scripture fulfilled in your ears.

God is saying: "I'm looking for history makers and I'm going to entrust former desolations to a generation of men and women today that want to inherit what became desolate in many generations before their time."

You can read more about the restoration God is going to do in one of my other books, Revelatory Restoration.

They shall repair the ruined cities, the desolations of many generations. When I heard the heart of God on this matter I stepped up and said, "God, I want to inherit and I will "step up to the plate" and inherit what has become a desolate heritage."

I realized that what we live in today, our accomplishments today can only be as great as the mothers and fathers and the shoulders that we stand on. The momentum that we have in the spirit is a momentum of prior generations. The momentum that our children's children receive is the momentum of prior generations based on how faithful we are to what we inherit in this generation from those that has gone before us. So it's like a compound blessing.

GENERATIONAL BLESSING & INHERITANCE

I want to give my spiritual children an inheritance from me in which the spiritual stature that I have matured into is where they start. The sons that have come under my ministry and the anointing of Revival Waves of Glory today will start their ministry from day one at the level that took me seven years to learn how to build. Many of them will never preach like I did in churches of 20 or 50 people because from day one they will be crusade evangelists.

It's sad that many fathers of the faith don't want to bring sons and daughters in on the level where they are functioning. We need to think differently!

God always thinks in terms of the generations that are to come. And God thinks from the beginning to the end and everything in between at the same time. God is already thinking about our children's children. Why don't we? We live for the now. Everything we make we spend. By the time we're finished, there's nothing for the kids we're not leaving an inheritance. We're not thinking "generations" and we're not considering generational blessings and inheritances. Here's how we think. When God gives us a prophetic word we think about it in the context of our life and ministry and how we're going to see this word come to pass in our lives and ministries. We don't think about it in terms of making our dreams and visions available to our children's children. We think about it in the context of, "Look what God gave me!" That's the way most of the church thinks, too. They haven't left much for the up-coming generation.

So the younger people come into the church and mostly all they find is religion and tradition. They understand that this isn't the way it should be and so they're trying to find their own way. They're struggling through because there are very few good examples of fathers today. But I want to store up an inheritance for my children's children so that when they step into the destiny of the Holy Ghost, they step into the same stature that I walk in today. They start with that. That's the only way we're going to go on and take the Promised Land. It's like their floor begins where my ceiling is. We need a new mindset!

Also we need to change our thinking in the area of God's timing. Here is a scripture verse that describes how God thinks.

Psalms 105:8 He hath remembered his covenant for ever, the word *which* he commanded to a thousand generations.

When God gives the word, He thinks about the word that He gives us in the context of a thousand generations.

However, when we receive a prophetic word and dream we get excited about it and can hardly wait for it to come to pass! Even if we lived until 120 years of age, does the dream and vision die with that person when they die? What if they never did see the fulfillment of the dream or promise? Can it become my dream? Can it become my children's dream and my children's, children's, children's, children's, up to a thousand generations?

How many of us have been excited about a prophetic word over our church? But at some point there is transition, the original leaders are gone and the church dies. So when that happens it looks like the prophetic word is gone, too. Or God gives a word over a city and we think, Oh God we've been waiting 50 years to do what You promised to do in our city. Most people never step into the prophetic word after the one who originally received the word dies or the church or ministry isn't operating anymore because we don't think in terms of generations.

We don't understand how the promise of God can be inherited even up to a thousand generations. So here's what I'm doing. As I said earlier, I'm looking for inheritances! For instance, I'm trying to find prophecies that Smith Wigglesworth gave so I can claim them for me, even though all the people he gave them to are dead and he's dead. But guess what? The prophetic word is not dead. God has given various powerful prophetic words hundreds of years ago. All the people involved in that word aren't alive anymore. But that word still stands waiting for a believer to find the old tape or manuscript and say, "Oh God, this one is 300 years old and I haven't seen it come to pass. I want to start living for this inheritance because everyone involved with that word is no longer alive to inherit it."

God is looking for those who are ready to stand up and say, "God, please give me the inheritance of generations that have become desolate." So I want us to think in terms of a thousand generations because when the prophetic word comes it's good for a thousand generations.

Even if God gives me a prophetic word and God forbid, I'm cut short in my prime, somebody needs to step up and take all my dreams and promises and continue on. And then even when they are dead and their children's children are dead, if someone doesn't know what God has promised me, then 500 years down the road that promise is forgotten and nobody inherits it and it's just available in the spirit realm. Think about that! This is deep stuff.

We usually think in terms of words that have come in the last 20 or 30 years. In fact, a generation is considered to be 30 years but what about the words that have come when a nation was formed? We can inherit those prophetic words today. God hasn't forgotten. His word is good for a thousand generations.

Psalms 33:11 The counsel of the LORD standeth for ever, the thoughts of his heart to all generations.

God thinks in terms of the generations. When God spoke to Abraham He saw Isaac. When God spoke to Isaac He saw Jacob and when He spoke to Jacob He saw Joseph.

When God saw Joseph He saw you and me because all the families of the earth are blessed in Abraham.

So when God spoke to Abraham it wasn't just a word to Abraham; it wasn't just a word to Isaac when

God spoke to him; it wasn't only Jacob's word, it was our word, too. That means that we can inherit today the same dreams and visions that God promised Abraham thousands of years earlier.

Genesis 12:3 And I will bless them that bless thee, and curse him that curseth thee: and in thee shall all families of the earth be blessed.

It was like God was saying that He wanted to bless the generations to come in the exact same way that He was blessing Abraham. Abraham was blessed!

There is a rich spiritual inheritance in Abraham! The first eight verses of Psalms 78 describe this generational mindset. Let's take a look at a few of these verses.

Psalms 78:5, 6 For he established a testimony in Jacob, and appointed a law in Israel, which he commanded our fathers, that they should make them known to their children: That the generation to come might know *them, even* the children *which* should be born; *who* should arise and declare *them* to their children:

At 37 years of age I'm thinking about my life, ministry and what I'm building but I'm already thinking about my children's children and what kind of inheritance I can leave them. I have a responsibility to these upcoming generations. The Bible says when God moves, He moves throughout the generations to a thousand generations! Having said that, it's the set time to start researching and reading some of the dreams and visions that God has promised. Ministries, cities and nations are sitting on inheritances. The plans and the counsel of the Lord stand for all generations. And so when we uncover what God has promised, that inheritance could become ours and we could start a new legacy from that day forward that will affect our children's children. We can inherit someone else's prophetic word, dream or vision!

Hallelujah!

Hebrews 1:7 And of the angels he saith, Who maketh his angels spirits, and his ministers a flame of fire.

Hebrews 1:14 Are they not all ministering spirits, sent forth to minister for them who shall be heirs of salvation?

Salvation is an inheritance. The Holy Spirit spoke to me that there are angels that are released right now like light.

Psalms 119:130 The entrance of thy words giveth light; it giveth understanding unto the simple.

God is saying that our inheritance will be souls! It's an inheritance that God gives to people, ministries and churches. And so I declare a whole new evangelistic anointing over the church. From this day forward we'll grow by souls. There is something about an inheritance of salvation coming to the church. We don't just want to have 500 new members in a church. We want to inherit 1,000 new souls. It's harvest time!

DOING THE STUFF!

Knowing the time and knowing the season that we're entering certainly colors our perspective! We want to inherit everything that the Lord has for us at this set time because God's kingdom is about to advance in an unparallel manner! Prophecies from the past few decades are coming to pass right now.

God is offering divine inheritances in the spirit, He's being redemptive. He wants to liberate and release prophetic destinies. It's time to start doing the stuff! We need to put actions to the dreams, prophetic words and prophetic visions and act like now is the time, not some unspecific time in the future. When God gives me a prophetic word I take it and, in my heart, it's "a go!" The moment I have a prophetic word, to me it means I have permission to go for it! God's going to redeem inheritances in this generation!

LEGAL RIGHTS TO A FAMILY INHERITANCE

We can begin inheriting God's promises today! So let's take a look at one of the places where inheritances can be found. I received revelation about this when the Holy Spirit spoke to me one day about restoring the desolation of many generations.

Inheritances are in our families and they are transmitted through the family.

Numbers 27:8-11 And thou shalt speak unto the children of Israel, saying, If a man die, and have no son, then ye shall cause his inheritance to pass unto his daughter. And if he have no daughter, then ye shall give his inheritance unto his brethren. And if he have no brethren, then ye shall give his inheritance unto his father's brethren. And if his father have no brethren, then ye shall give his inheritance unto his kinsman that is next to him of his family, and he shall possess it: and it shall be unto the children of Israel a statute of judgment, as the LORD commanded Moses.

Numbers 36:6-8 This *is* the thing which the LORD doth command concerning the daughters of

Zelophehad, saying, Let them marry to whom they think best; only to the family of the tribe of their father shall they marry. So shall not the inheritance of the children of Israel remove from tribe to tribe: for every one of the children of Israel shall keep himself to the inheritance of the tribe of his fathers. And every daughter, that possesseth an inheritance in any tribe of the children of Israel, shall be wife unto one of the family of the tribe of her father, that the children of Israel may enjoy every man the inheritance of his fathers.

There may be great preachers in your family that go back many years that you don't even know exist in your ancestry. What they labored for, you have the legal right to inherit so that you can begin to build on it. Some of you have forefathers who were missionaries. You can inherit their influence and favor because you are a direct descendant and you have the legal right to inherit their godly heritage.

If your great grandfather was a pastor at a small church or a big church, you may never want to pastor a church like they did, but why not collect their inheritance? It doesn't matter if they weren't well known. You have a legal right to those godly inheritances in your family tree.

Some of us know about our godly family history, but most of us never realized that we could inherit it. Others of us don't even know our family history. I don't even know about my family after the generation of my uncle and grandfather. We need to check out our individual family tree and history because there are probably some inheritances in our roots that we can claim. Let's receive as many inheritances as we can!

Also whether or not we have a legal family blood line connection with a forefather who had a godly heritage, we do have "in Christ" many brothers and sisters, fathers and mothers with heritages that are available in the spirit.

There aren't a lot of people that know about these inheritances and they don't realize that God thinks in terms of generations so a lot of the time, a mantle or an inheritance dies with the man or woman. For instance, there are 500 year old inheritances out there and because there aren't a whole lot of people looking for inheritances God is alerting us to the fact that these inheritances are available.

There are three characteristics in inheritances:
1) Material property,
2) Aspirations,
3) Words and promises.

When you are given a family divine inheritance, God gives you the same dream and the same word that He gave your father's father, and it becomes your prophetic word. Also, even if you have never received a prophetic word in your life, you can collect somebody else's prophetic words. Their inheritances (dreams, words and visions) still exist in heaven and whether God has given you any or not, you can just go ahead and collect theirs. So I am collecting words, dreams and visions. Every time a prophetic word is given for USA I take it. I claim it. Somebody else might claim it but I claim it too. It's going to be mine. I take the inheritance. Others can prophesy it but I am fulfilling it. I am the fulfillment of the word because I am inheriting the dreams and visions.

MANTLES ARE AVAILABLE, TOO!

God also wants us to know about the availability of different kinds of mantles. Some of the mantles belonged to great men and women of God. The Bible says that Enoch walked with God (Gen. 5:24). I believe Enoch's close relationship with God and his great character were reflected in his mantle, making it the shiniest.

Then the Lord said that Enoch's mantle was a main key to any other mantles being available to him. Then, because this young man's choice so pleased the Lord, it was like the Lord released to him an "unlimited invitation" to choose another mantle.

(We discussed the fact that mantles are found and received when God sees that we earnestly desire His highest will, His highest plan for our lives.) When our heart attitude is to walk with God like Enoch did then we are in the right position to receive a mantle from the Lord.

DIFFERENT KINDS OF INHERITANCES

Back to inheritances! I want to share different types of inheritances in the Bible.

The kingdom of God:
Matthew 25:34 Then shall the King say unto them on his right hand, Come, ye blessed of my Father, inherit the kingdom prepared for you from the foundation of the world:

There is an inheritance in the Bible called the kingdom of God. Believers in Jesus Christ will enter the kingdom and will see the kingdom of God but the Bible says also that there is an inheritance called the kingdom of God. Not everyone will inherit the kingdom of God, although everyone that knows Jesus Christ will enter the kingdom

64

of God. There is a difference. Some may enter the kingdom, but not inherit the kingdom. Some may enter the kingdom, but never inherit the kingdom in the land of the living because they didn't believe in miracles. It doesn't mean they won't get into heaven. It's just that they won't see the kingdom of God displayed on the earth.

God's promises:
Hebrews 6:12 That ye be not slothful, but followers of them who through faith and patience inherit the promises.

Through faith and patience we will inherit the promises of God.

Blessing:
1 Peter 3:9 Not rendering evil for evil, or railing for railing: but

contrariwise blessing; knowing that ye are thereunto called, that ye should inherit a blessing.

We inherit blessing.

The Glory:
Proverbs 3:35 The wise shall inherit glory: but shame shall be the promotion of fools.
We can inherit the glory and take possession of the glory.

And now I want to share inheritances in the blessing of Abraham. When God spoke to Abraham He saw each one of us because in Abraham all the families of the earth are blessed. So we can claim his inheritances in our day. God said to Abraham:

Genesis 12:2, 3 And I will make of thee a great nation, and I will bless thee, and make thy name great; and thou shalt be a blessing: And I will bless them that bless thee, and curse him that curseth thee: and in thee shall all families of the earth be blessed.

It's God's desire to make us, our family, ministry and church, a great nation and that we would enjoy fruitfulness and success. God wants to make nations out of our loins. We may only ever have two children but we can touch nations with the gospel!

It is possible to have hundreds of associate ministries, evangelists, prophets and apostles and then they produce and they produce and it just goes on!

Then it says, I will bless you and I will make your name great. You have a right to this in the spirit realm. God wants to make your name great. Exaltation! A good name and a good reputation.

Proverbs 22:1 A good name is rather to be chosen than great riches, and loving favour rather than silver and gold.

Ecclesiastes 7:1 A good name is better than precious ointment; and the day of death than the day of one's birth.

God wants to give you a name in which your name will precede you. Your name will be remembered throughout generations and your name will bring fear and holiness. Just the name of Israel brought dread to their enemies because God made their name great.

Genesis 35:5 And they journeyed: and the terror of God was upon the cities that *were* round about them, and they did not pursue after the sons of Jacob.

How about you, do you want to have a great name? It's important. God is into your name. This is for God's Glory

Another part of the inheritance is, you shall be blessed financially and you shall prosper so that you can be a blessing to others. Inheritances are also material. Look at Abraham.

Genesis 24:35 And the LORD hath blessed my master greatly; and he is become great: and he hath given him flocks, and herds, and silver, and gold, and menservants, and maidservants, and camels, and asses.

We can come into the inheritance of prosperity. God helped me to be faithful in little and then He brought the increase. I want to be a good steward over the things that God has given to this ministry.

I've been blessed with the revelation that I've got an inheritance and that it will always be in my family from this day forward!

Proverbs 19:14 House and riches *are* the inheritance of fathers: and a prudent wife *is* from the LORD.

Fathers, spiritual fathers, release inheritances and so as a father I want to declare that every associate ministry, every son and daughter that we raise up, every single one that graduates in our schools; they have a right to my inheritance because of association. I make a decree that from this day forward there will not be one Bill Vincent, not one associate ministry, not anyone that is ever a part of the nation that God gives me in the spirit that will ever lack any good thing that God wants them to have.

Psalms 34:10 The young lions do lack, and suffer hunger: but they that seek the LORD shall not want any good *thing.*

I am claiming my inheritance. Think that way. Just like Abraham was blessed, so am I and so are you!

Sometimes it's hard to relate to Abraham because he lived so many thousands of years ago. We are misguided if we can't accept what God has promised us in His word and if we try to wrap up God's word in our own ideas and prejudices. Some of the time our ideas are garbage, especially when it comes to walking in humility. Abraham was rich; that was the inheritance he had from God. This is what God said:

Genesis 12:2 And I will make of thee a great nation, and I will bless thee, and make thy name great; and thou shalt be a blessing:

Anything less is not God's fullness for our lives. God wants to give us the victory over our enemies.

Genesis 14:20 And blessed be the most high God, which hath delivered thine enemies into thy hand. And he gave him tithes of all.

The moment we claim the inheritance of Abraham we will be overcomers and our enemies will be delivered into our hand because of our association with Abraham. We will have the victory!

The manifest presence of God is a promise of the inheritance. The presence of God! That was part of the inheritance of Abraham.

Genesis 26:3 Sojourn in this land, and I will be with thee, and will bless thee; for unto thee, and unto thy seed, I will give all these countries, and I will perform the oath which I sware unto Abraham thy father;

Here is the promise of the inheritance of the presence of God again.

Genesis 28:15 And, behold, I *am* with thee, and will keep thee in all *places* whither thou goest, and will bring thee again into this land; for I will not leave thee, until I have done *that* which I have spoken to thee of.

The blessing of Abraham is material and financial blessing so that we can be a blessing. It means that our name will be great; we'll be a great nation, fruitful, enjoying the presence of God and driving out the enemy. Its victory, exaltation and favor!

RESTORATION OF UNFULFILLED INHERITANCES

Victory, exaltation and favor are God's will for us TODAY! He wants to bring restoration and renewal in everything that we've lost; every testimony, inheritance, dream and vision. I know God wants to bring restoration because last year I had an amazing encounter with the Father in a vision that changed my life about this whole matter.

I believe that God wants to take you into that place in the spirit today and show you what the inheritances are. The Psalmist said that those who delight themselves in the Lord,

God will grant to them the desires
of their heart (Ps. 37:4).

Power of Faith

God wants to release His awesome power through those who believe. This is a Chapter entitled: Faith and Power. In this Chapter I'll share about the secret to real faith that was revealed to me through personal deliverance. I will share a few more things that will stir your faith to believe God for what seems impossible. You'll receive some keys that will unlock tremendous breakthroughs as you pray for the sick and the lost. I didn't just wake up one day full of faith! As a matter of fact when I first got saved I was a real work in progress.

There were people in my town so mad at me I knew if I walked out at night there would be someone, somewhere, who would jump out of the dark to get me! But God wasn't going to leave me in that predicament and He truly took away my fear after one amazing supernatural achievement. I wouldn't allow myself to nod off until about five in the morning because I had to make sure I'd actually survive the night! I had knives and a baseball bat close by under my bed because there were death threats on my life from people who really did want to hurt me and kill me.

God showed up in my life supernatural and that experience broke off my fear and, as some would say, "I've never looked back." Today I am bold. Yet the kind of boldness I am talking about isn't all about a personality trait. We've all seen that raw, edgy boldness on certain people because of a rough life or other circumstances. That's not the kind of boldness I'm talking about. Rather it's a supernatural God-given boldness.

The apostles in Jesus' day needed that kind of boldness and they received it. So let's take a look at how they obtained supernatural boldness to continue the mighty works of God in the face of hatred and restrictions from the ultra-religious.

THE SECRET TO REAL FAITH

In the Book of Acts Chapter Three we read how the apostles were displaying God's power and then in Chapter Four how resistance and persecution broke out against them. They were forbidden to speak, to preach, or to teach in the name of Jesus. So they went to the Lord in prayer:

Acts 4:29-31 And now, Lord, behold their threatenings: and grant unto thy servants, that with all boldness they may speak thy word, By stretching forth thine hand to heal; and that signs and wonders may be done by the name of thy holy child Jesus. And when they had prayed, the place was shaken where they were assembled together; and they were all filled with the Holy Ghost, and they spake the word of God with boldness.

Although they were already moving in signs and wonders, the disciples realized that they needed something that only God could give by His Spirit. In other words, "God, we need something that's missing. Give us boldness!"

Now what happened next is absolutely remarkable:

Acts 4:31 And when they had prayed, the place was shaken where they were assembled together; and they were all filled with the Holy Ghost, and they spake the word of God with boldness.

When the Holy Spirit came upon the apostles a supernatural anointing of boldness came on them when they spoke the word of God. This is what we need in the church today! I'm talking about a supernatural anointing that you didn't have that comes on you, no matter what your personality type is. You get filled with the Spirit and you have a boldness you never had before. It's not about mustering up something that's not real or trying to be someone that you're not. Acts 4:33 And with great power gave the apostles witness of the resurrection of the Lord Jesus: and great grace was upon them all.

GREAT power and GREAT grace! Their faith was overflowing with GREAT substance.

The secret to real faith is: knowing that faith does not ultimately work to the max without boldness. Think about that. When boldness connects with faith, God's miracles happen!

Miracles make people bold. But first they have to get out of the boat, and that in itself takes a bold step of faith. But each step is God's training ground in the gift of faith. Supernatural Boldness, Obedience, and Faith brings God's Power. Truly, we need to be full of faith and boldness.

Do you know what makes a person bold? They've seen God's power manifested. It makes them bold, it makes them strong.

YOU'RE GOD'S MAN, YOU'RE GOD'S WOMAN!

All it takes is one sold-out ordinary man or woman wanting to be filled with supernatural boldness, full of faith and power, walking in obedience, to make a difference for God in this world. Just look at the apostle Stephen. He was an ordinary man with an extra-ordinary love for God.

Acts 6:3 Wherefore, brethren, look ye out among you seven men of honest report, full of the Holy Ghost and wisdom, whom we may appoint over this business.

Acts 6:5 And the saying pleased the whole multitude: and they chose Stephen, a man full of faith and of the Holy Ghost, and Philip, and Prochorus, and Nicanor, and Timon, and Parmenas, and Nicolas a proselyte of Antioch:

Acts 6:8 And Stephen, full of faith and power, did great wonders and miracles among the people.

Stephen was full of faith and power. I want to challenge some of you. I'm a "poster child" for God's grace! If God can transform someone like me and then work through me for His glory like He did for Stephen, He can do the same for you. Do you want to go full out for God? Or would you rather do your own thing? In simple terms, really, it comes down to this.

Church!! God wants way more for you than you just hiding out in your comfort zone.

The question is: Do you want all that God has for you? Do you really want to be full of faith and power?

For some of you this is a real turning point in your Christian life.

The Holy Spirit told me to write on what it takes to be full of faith and power for a reason. Please mark these words: THERE IS ANOTHER WAVE OF GOD'S MIRACULOUS POWER THAT IS ABOUT TO HIT THE CHURCH!

PREPARE FOR THE WAVE!

Any surfer will tell you that learning to catch a wave and then to successfully ride it takes determination, training, guts and preparation. After all, riding the waves like a pro doesn't just happen the first time a surfer paddles out to sea!

Likewise, before another wave of God's miraculous power hits the church, we believers will need that same grit determination, training, guts and preparation if we're going to flow with God's upsurge of power.

That's one of the main reasons why the Holy Spirit told me to teach about what it takes to be full of faith and power.

Doors and hearts are opening wide for the Gospel and God wants to send forth EQUIPPED laborers, like a well trained army, into the harvest fields. Hardy, seasoned, believers will successfully advance into and reap the harvest, and there is no time to waste.

Therefore today my goal in the rest of this Chapter is to more than simply wet your appetite for "a little something." My purpose and hope is to stir up such a hot fire in you that you'll be exploding with passion for what God is passionate about. For some of you it's time for a blazing inferno to be ignited within you for all that God wants for you being full of faith and power! IT IS TIME!

Let me tell you that faith comes by hearing. Next you need to know that faith is required for us to get going. These two aspects of faith really go hand in hand.

Romans 10:17 So then faith *cometh* by hearing, and hearing by the word of God.

Now let's take a look at the faith that gets us going.

In simple terms, this kind of faith happens when you know who you are in Christ and you know you can do what God says you can do. You believe it (who you are in Christ), act like it, and step out in faith that God will do what He said He would do. It is just raw faith.

Empowered with strength and authority—exousia [Greek word meaning: strength and authority, or right to use that power]

You just go and believe the Bible like it says,

Matthew 10:1 And when he had called unto *him* his twelve disciples, he gave them power *against* unclean spirits, to cast them out, and to heal all manner of sickness and all manner of disease.

Mark 16:17, 18 And these signs shall follow them that believe; In my name shall they cast out devils;

they shall speak with new tongues;
They shall take up serpents; and if
they drink any deadly thing, it shall
not hurt them; they shall lay hands
on the sick, and they shall recover.

I remember when God called me
to the ministry before I had any
anointing, before there was a
gifting, and before there was a gift
of faith. When I first stepped out all I
had was "go ye" faith "Let's believe
God in faith!" I just had a faith in the
Word, that's all. I didn't know
anything about angels or the word
of knowledge, open visions, the
supernatural, or the gift of faith. But
I believed all the great stories in the
Bible and I thought: God if you are
the same today as you were before
and will forever be, then anything is
possible!

Hebrews 13:8 Jesus Christ the same yesterday, and to day, and for ever.

My attitude was: "I am going to believe the Word.

I am going to put the principles of faith into action, step out and lay hands on the sick believing they will recover, and if they don't I am just going to keep praying anyways!"

My whole focus was "go ye," believing God's word, and I would think: The Holy Spirit confirms God's word, right? So if I get the word right, maybe some signs will follow. That's how my healing ministry began even though there were hardly any results! However, during this time of testing, God was setting up a sequence of events that would not only give results but they would also launch me into one of my first supernatural encounters.

The Lord actually challenged me big time when I was preaching my heart out on radical faith during a meeting. Suddenly I felt compelled to ask the small crowd: "Who believes God for a miracle?"

A Woman that was a missionary was bound with rheumatoid arthritis. I told her she was being healed and went on with the meeting. I saw her months later and she was totally healed and ready to go back to the mission field.

Matthew 10:8 Heal the sick, cleanse the lepers, raise the dead, cast out devils: freely ye have received, freely give.

So we need to believe what God says in the Bible and go!

The Bible also says to "raise the dead." Matthew 10:8 Heal the sick, cleanse the lepers, raise the dead, cast out devils: freely ye have received, freely give.

Yet, I have learned through past experience that raising the dead differs from healing the sick. By that I mean, healing the sick is just "heal the sick" it's praying for everyone, all the time. But not necessarily so for raising the dead! God never promised all the dead would be raised. But the dead do get raised. Although I will still pray in faith for someone to be resurrected, I now realize that raising the dead "takes the voice of God."

It's important that you take to heart that when you are full of the Holy Spirit, the gift of faith is within you, and what's more, your boldness is the key to release that faith. Remember I said that the secret to real faith is: knowing that faith does not ultimately work to the max without boldness. In fact, if you and I are willing to risk it all, we will operate in full faith and power. Why? It's because God wants us to! Conversely, until you and I can risk it all, we'll fail to operate in full faith and power. Why? Because as I shared at the beginning of this segment; there is another wave of God's miraculous power that's about to hit the church. If we're only willing to operate minimally then we aren't in the right position to flow with God's coming upsurge of power.

My hope and prayer is that you will step out and just "do it" and not give up until something happens. Countless believers have done just that and can testify to God's glory about what they have witnessed, just like I have in this teaching series. All because it's about Jesus! He is our focus! Any miracle that God ever does is all for the glory of His Son, Jesus Christ!

Raise the Dead

There is a level of faith that causes the dead to live. The Bible says it's elementary. This is a Chapter that we all need in the Church. I have been given divine revelations from the Holy Spirit and I believe we will see many resurrections in America and across the world.

John 11:1-5 Now a certain *man* was sick, *named* Lazarus, of Bethany, the town of Mary and her sister Martha. (It was *that* Mary which anointed the Lord with ointment, and wiped his feet with her hair, whose brother Lazarus was sick.) Therefore his sisters sent unto him, saying, Lord, behold, he whom thou lovest is sick. When

Jesus heard *that,* he said, This sickness is not unto death, but for the glory of God, that the Son of God might be glorified thereby. Now Jesus loved Martha, and her sister, and Lazarus.

He emphasizes it twice. Jesus loved Martha, loved her sister and loved Lazarus. He was passionately in love with Lazarus. He cared about all the needs of his life. When He heard that he was sick, about the depression, the impossible circumstances, and the impossible needs of Lazarus, He stayed two more days in the place where He was. Lazarus was not just sick; He was on his deathbed. He did not need Jesus tomorrow; he needed Jesus yesterday. We are talking about an impossible circumstance. There are dead ministries God wants to raise. There are dead visions that God wants to raise. There are people who are dead in their bodies with sickness and disease. God wants to raise the dead. There are those who are giving up in their hearts right now. They are on the verge of financial breakthrough. Some who are called are giving up right now in the area of ministry in the vision of God and are on the verge of one of the most glorious days and release of the anointing that they would ever walk in. How do we know that today is not the day for our miracle?

How do we know that the sun is not going to rise tomorrow? How do we know that today, for the infirmity that someone has had for thirty-eight years, will not be the day that God says, "Be made whole?"

We need to live every day of our lives with new mercies. We need to live every day of our lives as if today is the day. Today could be the day that He says, "Do you want to be made whole?" Have you been in that place in your life where just when you thought the light and the breaking of the dawning of a new day was coming, and it could not get darker, it got darker? The car broke down, you lost your job, and you went, "That's ok, I've got some money in the savings account".

And you got home and said, "OK Lord, if anything else is going to happen, I'm going to absolutely snap". Then you find out that the other vehicle you had, your son crashed, and the washing machine broke down, and somebody robbed your bank. Your money is gone and they do not know if they are going to be able to get it back. It always seems like it gets darker before the light comes. Just when you think the light is going to come and that it cannot get any darker, all of a sudden it gets more impossible. Another hardship and another trial comes, and you say, "God I'm not going to be able to take any more". The pressures of life mount up even more. Do you know what I am talking about? Are you at that place? Do you need something raised from the dead? Do you need a spiritual breakthrough? Are you ready for the release of resurrection power?

JESUS' PERSPECTIVE

John 11:7-15 Then after that saith he to *his* disciples, Let us go into Judaea again. *His* disciples say unto him, Master, the Jews of late sought to stone thee; and goest thou thither again? Jesus answered, Are there not twelve hours in the day? If any man walk in the day, he stumbleth not, because he seeth the light of this world. But if a man walk in the night, he stumbleth, because there is no light in him. These things said he: and after that he saith unto them, Our friend Lazarus sleepeth; but I go, that I may awake him out of sleep. Then said his disciples, Lord, if he sleep, he shall do well. Howbeit Jesus spake of his death: but they thought that he had spoken of taking of rest in sleep. Then said Jesus unto them plainly, Lazarus is dead. And I am glad for your sakes that I was not there, to the intent ye may believe; nevertheless let us go unto him.

Do you notice something about the perspective of Jesus? Lazarus was dead, but Jesus said he was sleeping. Was Jesus lying? God does not see our circumstances the way we see them. God does not see cancer and incurable diseases the way that we see them. God does not see the impossibilities of life the way that we see them. In your heart, you may think your marriage is dead, your finances are dead, your ministry is dead, the anointing is dead, or your reputation is dead. You may have a vision in your heart that has died. There may have been a time when you dreamed about great exploits, and now your hope is dead. The Lord said, "It is not dead, it is sleeping". The perspective of God sees our present circumstances and needs different than we do. And if it is sleeping, "I go that I may wake it up." We need to speak to our situation and say it is not dead, it is sleeping. Though we have backslidden sons and daughters, and unsaved family, it does not mean that they are dead. To God, they are sleeping. There is something about the heart of God that likes to move in the impossible. There is something about the heart of God that likes to move when something is dead. There is something about breakthrough and the dawning of a new day that comes when you are so dead and hopeless that you do not know if anything is going to be able to happen.

That is when God is going to come. He said, "Lazarus is dead and I am glad for your sakes, that I was not there." Why am I glad for your sakes? I am glad for your sakes that you might believe. Every time that you are in a place where you no longer have the strength and the ability in your own gifting and theology, and you have come to the place where you are so empty and broken that you cannot move, say, "God says it is opportunity. That which is dead is opportunity for resurrection." Martha said, "Lord, if You had been here, my brother would not have died." And Jesus said, "I am the resurrection and the life." She said, "I know You are the resurrection and the life. My brother is going to rise. I am going to see him again at the Second Coming. I am going to see my brother again in heaven." And Jesus said, "I AM!".... "I AM!" .... "I AM!" Today He says, "I AM, right now, I AM the resurrection of that which is dead. I AM. Not, I am tomorrow. I AM the resurrection and the life." And she said, "But even now I know that whatever You ask of God, God will give You."

Just like you and me. It is easy whenever we have victory under our belt. We are walking in the victory of God, or we are in the mountain of breakthrough. There is faith and assurance. We are speaking to the mountain and it is moving. Breakthrough is in our life. We are overcoming. We say, "God, whatever You ask, I'll believe it. Lord, I have faith right now for the impossible. I have faith right now to move mountains. I can raise the dead!"

Have you been in the place where just when you have victory under your belt, the phone rings? Lazarus is dead. All hope that you had for your circumstance is dead. And God says, "I am glad". Because it is not dead, it is sleeping. And if it is sleeping, I go that I may wake it up.

Martha said, "I know, even though I know my brother is dead, whatever You ask of God, He will give it to You. " He said, "Your brother will rise again." He said, "Let me see if you really believe what you say you believe. You say that whatever I ask of God, He is going to give it. Let me just test this thing and say, Your brother is going to rise again."

We take the Word of God and put it in the future. "I am going to be healed." "I am going to die and go to heaven. Everything is always tomorrow. I am a "now" kind of a kingdom guy. Today is the day of salvation. If I saw it in the Word of God, it was yesterday, and I should have applied it already. I live in the place that if it is there, I am going to have it now. And that is why we have been able to come to where we are so quickly. We refuse to wait. I believe in the patience of God, and the timing of God, but there are certain things that I refuse to wait on. If I know it is "now", if I know it was "yesterday", I am not going to wait. I am going to have it today. I am going to do everything that I can to lay hold of that which Christ has laid hold of for me, until I see it.

If miracles are now, then I am going to have miracles. I am not going to wait. You are never going to have a healing ministry. You have a healing ministry. You are never going to have an evangelism ministry. You have an evangelism ministry. You are to win souls now.

Too many evangelists I know in the body of Christ do not even remember the last time they prayed and led anyone to Jesus. And you are an evangelist? How can an evangelist not win souls? Whether you are an evangelist now or an evangelist in ten years, you were an evangelist when God ordained you in the womb. So start acting like one. I have this "Now, Kingdom" kind of idea. And we need to lay hold of that which God has laid hold of for us.

Jesus reached the tomb. Lazarus was dead for four days in the grave, and his body had begun to smell. "Jesus wept." Do you know why Jesus wept? Some people believe that He wept because He had such a heart of compassion for Lazarus. He saw Martha, He saw Mary. He wept because He was grieving and mourning because Lazarus was dead.

Jesus was not weeping because of compassion. Jesus groaned in His Spirit and wept because of the state of unbelief of His people.

When it really comes down to where the rubber hits the road and the Lord says to us, "I AM the Resurrection", it is always tomorrow. We cannot lay hold of what God has for us now. But faith lays hold of the promise NOW!

"I hope I get healed." "I hope its coming". "I hope this is it, Bill" "I hope that was the word of knowledge." God wants us to have hope. But do not allow your hope to be defined as "not until tomorrow." Faith lays hold of things now. Faith takes it as if it is yours, even if you do not see it. That is the substance of faith. He groaned in His Spirit because of the unbelief. They did not recognize the power that Jesus had over that which was dead and impossible. He looked at Martha after He had raised Lazarus from the dead and He said, "Did I not tell you that if you would believe, you would have seen the glory of God?" But you did not believe what you said you believed. So, I am glad that Lazarus is dead. Because now the deadness in Lazarus' body is an opportunity for me to show you that what is impossible with man is not impossible with God.

LEVELS OF HEALING ANOINTING

About three years ago, I started to get real excited about miracles. I had visitations from the Lord that lasted at times up to twelve hours with me on the carpet. I started to have trips in the Spirit. Out of that season, the word of knowledge and healing began to be released. When I first began to be released in healing, I had faith for backs. I had a little faith for pain in peoples' bodies. So I began to lay hands on the sick and pray for backs to be healed and for pain to come out of peoples' bodies. As people got healed, I gained authority for the backs. I grew in a place of faith and confidence for the back. So you can kind of say that in the beginning of my healing ministry, I had a back-healing ministry. I said, "God, I am ready to see a few more miracles. I want to see a little bit more of the creative. So the Lord began to give me faith for limbs, legs or arms that were a little bit shorter than others, to grow out a couple of inches.

I got excited, and started to pray and believe for stomach conditions. I started to have faith for different categories of sickness and diseases. We like to categorize some things as harder than others. We think it is harder to heal cancer than asthma, and it is harder to heal cancer than backs. It is not true, but that is what we do.

So then, I started to have faith for cancer. I said, "Now I am going to get some authority in the Spirit over cancer, and the devil is going to know and I am going to know. I am going to walk in a new place and be able to get people healed of cancer.

WARRING AND CONTENDING
FOR THE MIRACULOUS

MarK 5:21-23 And when Jesus was passed over again by ship unto the other side, much people gathered unto him: and he was nigh unto the sea. And, behold, there cometh one of the rulers of the synagogue, Jairus by name; and when he saw him, he fell at his feet, And besought him greatly, saying, My little daughter lieth at the point of death: *I pray thee,* come and lay thy hands on her, that she may be healed; and she shall live.

Here is perfect faith. "Come lay your hands on her and she will live." If I can get a hold of you now, God, she will live. I have perfect faith and confidence.

Why is it that God likes to come through at the last minute? When I get to heaven, I am going to ask God about this. Why is it that God is never early, but He is never late? Before the breakthrough comes, we think He is late. Then we see it come and realize how perfect He was. Then we vow, next time, next time, and next time I am going to have faith. God is never early. Why can He not bring breakthrough early to those who are living by faith? What is it about God and the last hour? What is it about God with the dead? What is it about God with the impossible? What is it about God that He hears about the circumstances of your life and He waits two more days? Why does He bring you to that place? "Because; I am glad for your sakes that you might believe I want you to conquer some things. I want to put some levels in your Spirit."

Mark 5:35 While he yet spake, there came from the ruler of the synagogue's *house certain* which said, Thy daughter is dead: why troublest thou the Master any further?

He was still giving the confession of faith. He was still in a place of confidence. He said, "Whatever You ask of God, He will give it." If you will come now, God, I will have my breakthrough. It will happen, Lord. If you lay Your hands on my daughter, she will live. Have you been there? "My breakthrough is coming. I have hold of God. I can feel it. I have it in the Spirit. The victory is coming. And then all of a sudden...While He was speaking, one of the rulers came and said, "Your daughter is dead". Pop! There goes the balloon of your faith, enthusiasm, and excitement. When you thought it could not get any more impossible, it got more impossible. And God says, "I am glad for your sakes." Because, that which is dead is opportunity for My resurrection power. We need to get excited about that which is dead.

Mark 5:36 As soon as Jesus heard the word that was spoken, he saith unto the ruler of the synagogue, Be not afraid, only believe.

This man came to the crossroad of faith. God said if a miracle is going to happen, I must keep this man in faith. I must keep him believing that it is just as easy for Me to heal his daughter now, even though she is dead as it was for Me to heal her when she was alive. I must move My church into the place where they know that it is just as easy for Me to heal a blind eye as it is for Me to heal a back condition. I must bring My church to a revelation that it does not take more sweat to stretch forth My hand and heal somebody in a wheelchair than it does for Me to heal somebody's stomach condition. I must keep him in that place where he is going to believe, because faith is going to release this miracle. He said, "Only believe". If you can still believe the way you believed a moment ago, even though it seems even more impossible now when she is dead, I can still release your miracle. But it is so important that you only believe.

Only believe. That is easy to say, isn't it? Only believe. I mean, let me make it simple. Only Believe. You do not have a choice. There is no other choice. Only Believe. Do you know what the Bible gives you? The

Bible gives you these three things; faith, hope and love. You do not even have the right to choose to be discouraged. You do not have the right not to believe. So you might as well just purpose in your heart today that you have faith, hope, and love.

God did not require anything of you except to believe. How long must I believe for my healing God? It has been years. Great men of God have prayed for me. The church has prayed for me, and I am still not healed.

God did not say ten years, twelve years, or thirty-eight years. He said, "Many died not yet having received the promise". That means that you must war for what God wants to give you. If you do not have it, you war for it until you get it, or until the day that you die. You must war for it until your last breath. There is nothing else but faith, hope and love.

You just might as well make a purpose in your heart today that you are going to have to war. We are going to have to contend. We have to get excited about that which looks dead and say, "It is not dead, it is only sleeping."

THE FAITH OF ABRAHAM

Do you know why Abraham is known as the Father of Faith? The Bible says in Romans 4 that Abraham called forth those things that were not as though they were, and believed that God could give life to the dead.

God told Abraham as He tested him, "I want you to bring your only son and kill him. I want you to give me Isaac." Abraham was like you and I.

He probably laid up all night and thought, "How am I going to tell Sarah that I have to take Isaac and kill him? What are the neighbors going to think? How can I justify taking the son of my own flesh? How am I going to take Isaac up there? How am I going to tie him up and take that knife and kill him? What if I have to stab him three times? What if he doesn't die right away? What if it hurts and I miss the fatal organ or something? That cannot be God. God said that in me all of the nations of the earth were going to be blessed. Isaac is the only natural manifestation that can even possibly help me get from point A to point B. If I take him out of the way, then what God promised cannot happen. So, this cannot be God."

He probably started to reason. And you better believe that he was like you and I. I mean, he loved his son. And he may have laid there all night long thinking about that. But, let me show you what happened. Abraham counted God as a God to give life to the dead. Somewhere along the line, Abraham saw himself kill Isaac and saw God raise him from the dead.

He knew that even if he brought Isaac unto that mountain and took his life. God would just raise him from the dead. And when he actually got up on the mountain, God said, "Because you already saw it and you already did it in the Spirit, it is as good as done."

Your miracle begins in your spirit. You need to see it. As you see it as done, it will manifest. You need to see it as finished. Abraham thought, "I already see Isaac killed, dead, and raised up. God gives life to the dead and calls forth those things which are not. If I bring him up there and kill him, God will resurrect him". We must see it in our Spirit. We must catch a vision and revelation of what Jesus has already done. We must see ourselves healed.

IT BEGINS WITH A SEED

2 Kings 4:14 And he said, What then *is* to be done for her? And

Gehazi answered, Verily she hath
no child, and her husband is old.
And she said to her husband, "Look
now, I know that this is a holy man
of God, who passes by us regularly.

"Please, let us make a small
upper room on the wall; and let us
put a bed for him there, and a table
and a chair and a lampstand; so it
will be, whenever he comes to us,
he can turn in there. And it
happened one day that he came
there, and he turned into the upper
room and laid down there. Then he
said to Gehazi his servant, "Call this
Shunammite woman". When he had
called her, she stood before him.

And he said to him, "Say now to
her, 'Look, you have been
concerned for us with all this care.
What can I do for you? Do you want

me to speak on your behalf to the king or to the commander of the army?'" She answered, "I dwell among my own people."

So he said, "What then is to be done for her?" And Gehazi answered, "Actually, she has no son, and her husband is old." So, he said, "Call her". When he had called her she stood in the doorway. Then he said, "About this time next year you shall embrace a son." And she said, "No, my lord.

Man of God, do not lie to your maidservant". See, there was such hopelessness; such despair in her heart because she had tried for so many years to have a child. So many healing evangelists had already prayed for her that she did not want to hear something that sounded too good to be true. She said, "Lord, I have heard this too many times. Do not lie to your maidservant. You do not understand the wound in my heart. God, I am tired. I have been battling this allot of years."

She did not get excited and say, "God said it and I believe it. Whatever you ask of God, He will do it. Whatever I ask in prayer believing, I receive it, hallelujah. I lay hold of that promise. It is mine. I am talking as if it is mine before I even have it." But something happened. This is what happens to you when God does what He says He is going to do. It releases confidence and faith.

2 Kings 4:17 And the woman conceived, and bare a son at that

season that Elisha had said unto her, according to the time of life.

She had the manifestation of the promise of God. Have you ever had the manifestation of what God promised and the very thing that God gave you was taken away? And you said, "My God, I thought it came from You. I do not understand. I thought you were the One who led me to plant this church and now it is dead. I had the Word of God and saw the manifestation. I walked for a season in that gift, but now it is dead!"

2 Kings 4:18-20 And when the child was grown, it fell on a day, that he went out to his father to the reapers. And he said unto his father, My head, my head. And he said to a lad, Carry him to his

mother. And when he had taken him, and brought him to his mother, he sat on her knees till noon, and *then* died.

I can see the transformation of the spirit of this woman. "No, Man of God, do not lie to me. Do not tell me things that are too good to be true. I have had so many prophecies. I do not want another prophetic word." But there was a transformation that happened in her heart.

2 Kings 4:21-23 And she went up, and laid him on the bed of the man of God, and shut *the door* upon him, and went out. And she called unto her husband, and said, Send me, I pray thee, one of the young men, and one of the asses, that I may run to the man of God,

and come again. And he said, Wherefore wilt thou go to him to day? *it is* neither new moon, nor sabbath. And she said, *It shall be* well.

Every time you purpose to believe God, every time you purpose to run to the man of God, every time you purpose to lay hold of the promise that God spoke to you, somebody will come to you and say, "Why are you going after the man of God today? It is not God's will. How do you know that God wants to heal you? God does not want to heal all. I have tried to get healed for twelve years. What makes you think that you are going to get healed? You have the same affliction as I. I am more righteous than you. There is more sin in your life. I have not gotten healed.

Who gave you the right to expect to get healed? Come on, it's not the new moon, it's not the Sabbath." There is always some voice, some preacher, some family, and some friend that cannot see it the way that you do. See when you have something in your spirit; nobody can have it except you. Nobody can understand where you are going except you. How could I go in just a few years from being a drug addict to doing Prophetic Crusades? I had something in my spirit. See, something happened to this woman. She believed the Word of God and she went after the man of God. "It is well. He is not dead, he is sleeping. I cannot see it now, but it is well."

2 Kings 4:24-27 Then she saddled an ass, and said to her servant, Drive, and go forward; slack not *thy* riding for me, except I bid thee. So she went and came unto the man of God to mount Carmel. And it came to pass, when the man of God saw her afar off, that he said to Gehazi his servant, Behold, *yonder is* that Shunammite: Run now, I pray thee, to meet her, and say unto her, *Is it* well with thee? *is it* well with thy husband? *is it* well with the child? And she answered, *It is* well. And when she came to the man of God to the hill, she caught him by the feet: but Gehazi came near to thrust her away. And the man of God said, Let her alone; for her soul *is* vexed within her: and the LORD hath hid *it* from me, and hath not told me.

Elisha said, "I am a prophet, but the Holy Spirit has shown me nothing about the deadness of her son. I know nothing about the impossibility of her circumstance." He does not know that her son is dead. The Lord has hidden it from him. Yet, the very thing that God tells him to ask that woman is what God heard her say moments ago at her house. See, God is listening to what we say with our mouth. And there is always going to come a place where He is going to challenge us to see if we really believe what we say we believe. Because, Martha said, "Lord, whatever You ask of God, He is going to give it. He said, "Oh yeah? Your brother will rise again." She said, "I know, one day…"

He said, "No! I am the resurrection and the life!" And until the Word of the Lord comes to pass in your life, the Word of the Lord will test you. When you have a confession of faith, you better get ready for everything in hell to come against what you say and that which you have seen in your spirit. It is on the way.

God heard the woman say to her servant, "It will be well." I believe a miracle is on the way. I purpose in my heart and refuse to allow those discouraging voices to say, "It's not the time, it's not the new moon, it's not the Sabbath. No I have seen it in my spirit and I'm going after the Word of God. The Word of God is my answer. The promise of God is my answer. God is my answer and

I'm going to lay hold of God and I'm going to be urgent about it.

Now she is in her trial for a while. She has had time to let it sink in that she is in an impossible circumstance. Her son is dead. So the Lord wanted to say, "Do you still believe the way that you believed moments ago?" He said, "Is it well with you?" It is like He was saying, "Only believe. Do you still believe it? Is it well with you? Is it well with your child? Is it well with your husband?" She said, "It is well." And she lay hold of the feet of the man of God and said, "Did I not tell you not to lie to me?" What she did was lay hold of the man that represented the Word of God and she said, "Have You not said, God? Does not Your Word declare, God? Have You not promised, God? Is this not Your Word to me? I got hold of You and I'm not going to let go, regardless of what I feel or see. I believe if You spoke it, it shall still be. And it will be well, though I don't see it now, though it's dead now, it's only sleeping. And if it's sleeping, I go that I might wake it up. It's not impossible. It just looks impossible for the moment. But I am glad for your sakes, because that which is dead is an opportunity for you to reach the realm of the impossible, the miraculous and the resurrection power of God.

2 Kings 4:29-31 Then he said to Gehazi, Gird up thy loins, and take my staff in thine hand, and go thy way: if thou meet any man, salute him not; and if any salute thee, answer him not again: and lay my staff upon the face of the child. And

the mother of the child said, *As* the LORD liveth, and *as* thy soul liveth, I will not leave thee. And he arose, and followed her. And Gehazi passed on before them, and laid the staff upon the face of the child; but *there was* neither voice, nor hearing. Wherefore he went again to meet him, and told him, saying, The child is not awaked.

There was no voice. There was no hearing. I went to a crusade and believed God. I got excited months before I got to that crusade, and hands were laid on me. I felt nothing. There was no change. There was no voice. There was nothing. I left the same as I had come. I came four nights to that miracle crusade, and I still left sick. People have prayed for me for ten years. There is still no voice. There is still no hearing.

Elisha sent this man. Think about the expectation, the faith and the excitement of that woman's heart. The prophet gave the word. This is Elisha. The guy went with the staff. She could just about taste her victory. And then he came back and said, "Oh, nothing happened, might as well go home I didn't get healed.

The best of the best have prayed for me. I'm still sick. I might as well give up." God gave us faith, hope and love. Many died not yet receiving the promise. There is no other choice in the kingdom but to believe and war until we are dead! Get it in your heart to say no to hopelessness and discouragement. It is time to purpose in your heart that you have no other choice but to hold on to the Word of God and the promise of God… or die. Which one is it going to be? Die or believe God?

2 Kings 4:32-34 And when Elisha was come into the house, behold, the child was dead, *and* laid upon his bed. He went in therefore, and shut the door upon them twain, and prayed unto the LORD. And he went up, and lay upon the child, and put his mouth upon his mouth, and his eyes upon his eyes, and his hands upon his hands: and he stretched himself upon the child; and the flesh of the child waxed warm.

The prophet prayed two times. He still did not get raised from the dead. So Elisha jumped up off of his bed and prayed a third time. And he stretched himself out over that boy again and said "life". After the third time, the boy was raised from the dead. It happened to Elijah too. The third time that Elijah prayed for the widow's son, he raised up from the grave.

Miracles did not just happen for me. I had to war, contend, conquer, war, contend, conquer, put my faith out, and I am still not where I am going to be in the miraculous. But I am still contending. I am still saying, "My God, I'm not satisfied. I'm putting my faith out there for more." I am still giving myself to praying for the impossible and I am still warring, contending, and pushing. I have a level, but I am not satisfied.

You may receive in a conference the seed of healing. It is the beginning of the manifestation of your miracle. But it is going to be released. Your flesh might get warm and you still might not be healed. Someone may lay hands on you and there may be no voice, no hearing, and no sign that anything has happened. My message is a little bit different. It is okay to fight. It is okay to contend. It is okay not to be healed. It is okay not to be fully manifested in your miracle. The prayer of faith is "birthing it".

When Jesus raised Lazarus from the dead, He did not have to lay hands on the dead. There was authority in the Word of God. What is dead? Maybe your faith is dead. Maybe your relationship with God is dead. Maybe your marriage is dead. Maybe your body is dead. Maybe your church is dead. Maybe your ministry is dead. Maybe your children are dead. I want you to stretch yourself out in the spirit over them. I want you to see it, and command resurrection power to be released. Why are you disquieted within me, oh soul? Why are you cast down? I do not have any other choice! I will hope in God! Who are you, soul, to rule me? Rule your soul! Why are you cast down in me, my emotions, my will, and my mind? It is hope or die. So be renewed in faith. Let your faith be resurrected. Let warfare be released for warring and contending for miracles are released in the Name of Jesus Christ. Let your vision be resurrected, let hopelessness and despair GO in the Name of Jesus! Because remember it is well. It is well!

Power in the Blood

The blood of Jesus is still alive and has power. As I go through my own time of healing, restoration, and growth, I realize how fervently the devil tries to detour us from knowing Christ and from growing in Christ. Satan's plan is to take our eyes off Jesus and minimize the impact and transforming power of His shed blood to steer us away from the course of the path God has for us, not to hurt us as much as his plan is to hurt God. The enemy is determined to tempt us, lure us, entice us, and persuade us to sin because it hurts the Father when we do. The devil is determined that we suffer, that we are sick and in pain, because God suffers when His children suffer. No one feels pain more than a parent whose child is sick, lost, or depressed, whose teen is rebellious or distant, a runaway or wayward son or daughter.

A parent feels the pain and if he or she could take that pain upon themselves if it would remove it from the child. Our heavenly Father did just that, His only Son, Jesus Christ of Nazareth, obediently and willingly shed His blood, which was powerful enough to save, heal, and deliver every person on the planet, whosoever believes, all at once and in an instant billions and billions of people the overcoming power of His resurrected life establishing forever eternally the irrefutable power of His precious blood.

The richness of His grace and the blood shed was more than enough to transform your life.

Ephesians 1:7 In whom we have redemption through his blood, the forgiveness of sins, according to the riches of his grace;

Ephesians 2:13 But now in Christ Jesus ye who sometimes were far off are made nigh by the blood of Christ.

If you do not know Jesus, or are far off, I want you to know right now that the battle is on in the supernatural realm to prevent you coming to Christ. Salvation is a serious battle because once you align with Jesus and apply the saving, healing, forgiving, redemptive, pure miraculous substance to your life, the devil, his demons, and his plans are bound, restrained, and defeated, and your life and everything within your life can transform for the glory of God. Satan hates and fears the blood of Jesus. He cannot fight its power and he cannot counterfeit it. When we apply the blood of Jesus to our lives, just as we did in salvation, the enemy knows without a doubt, he is defeated. Just one drop of His blood applied in faith, can heal your family or a nation!

If you are reading this and you do not know Jesus you just can't understand why you need a Savior; you cannot see salvation as a way to God; the Bible just doesn't make sense to you, or, you do not think you are worth saving trust that the devil has blinded you because God loves you, desires a personal relationship with you, and has an eternal plan for your life.

The devil wants to break God's heart by keeping you away from Him. I encourage you, before you even read further into this message, to visit our website www.revivalwavesofglory.com and click on the tab, "Salvation," without further argument, and I pray now for that veil to be lifted, in Jesus' name. Then hurry back, because the rest of this message is about how the very blood that He shed for you and His overcoming resurrection power can empower your life, from here on in!

TAP INTO POWER

We do not tap into the power of the blood of Jesus near often enough for healing or deliverance, for our physical and heart ailments, for empowerment and peace of mind in this life. Some people wrongly assume that the blood grants us immunity from these things, or others, that the blood dried up a thousand years ago! Not! We have an immeasurable supply to apply in resurrection power in the name of Jesus to our circumstances! Satan's plan is to destroy and kill us, and daily we are in the midst of battle.

But I am training and equipping my hands for victory, thank You Jesus! The devil is a loser. He lost his greatest battle to Jesus at Calvary. Christ's victory forced Satan to give up the keys of Hades and death. Not only has Satan already lost ground the Kingdom of Heaven continues to gain ground on him! Daily, there are battles but the biggest battle Christ won, thus I can pray out of victory, out of a victorious mind-set.

POWER TO LIVE AS OVERCOMERS

Would you like to see the devil and his demons run? Talk about the blood! Read Bible Scriptures about the blood aloud and the devil and his demons will flee.

Revelations 12:11 And they overcame him by the blood of the Lamb, and by the word of their testimony; and they loved not their lives unto the death.

If I need to deal with demons that manifest in my meetings, I speak and read God's Word about the blood.

I tell you, sometimes I don't even have time to take authority over Satan's minions because they run, like the devil at the mere mention of the power of Christ's blood, and then people receive healing and deliverance! It is remarkable that they (the brethren) overcame the devil by the blood of the Lamb. They also overcame his workings and assignments. How did they do that? Note, the verse does not say, "We have overcome," but rather, "They overcame him." It is something they had to do an action an application of the blood in their lives. That is what we need to learn too; how to overcome the enemy by the blood of the Lamb, the blood shed at Calvary 2000 years ago. Why do we not always overcome the enemy in the trials and battles of today? I endeavor because although many of us are aware of the blood and are thankful for it, we do not use it! We often cannot get past the fact that Jesus shed His blood so long ago but what about the power of His blood today. What about reaching toward Heaven for it and applying it in your life? How do you apply it? Speak and use the blood in your circumstances, right there in the front lines of your battle with the enemy.

Understanding the Preciousness of the Blood Key!

Isaiah 52:14 As many were astonied at thee; his visage was so marred more than any man, and his form more than the sons of men:

Never was any man's face more marred or his form more altered and disfigured than Christ's face was. They rearranged it His nose and eyes were not where they should be. He became unrecognizable. His entire body bled from the brutal scourging. They shouted, "Prophesy to us, Christ!" and the interrogators beat Him. Every one of the 39 lashes He endured at the hands of the Roman soldiers ripped out chunks of skin so large, people stared at His exposed bones.

Psalms 22:17 I may tell all my bones: they look *and* stare upon me.

Blood completely covered Jesus from the very top of His head, to His toes. Every inch of Him bled.

His back looked like ground hamburger meat with spinal vertebrae showing through and the blood poured out and down His legs. On that precious savagely whipped back, and with bones exposed, He carried His own cross to Golgotha. That 60 to 80 pound rough log painfully rubbed against and chafed His bare and raw back as He carried it to die for the sins of the world. Blood gushed from the wounds on His head and face, His body, and His back, and then out of the nail piercings in His hands and His feet on the cross. He must have lost most of His blood by the time He actually died at Calvary. Blood shed for the remission of sin so that we could be forgiven. Blood shed so that we could again walk in the Garden with Him. Blood shed to restore intimacy. Blood shed so that we could experience the manifest presence of God. Blood shed so we could experience His touch, His healing, His goodness, His love, and His forgiveness. Blood shed so we could reconcile with Him. Blood shed for redemption. Blood shed to disarm powers and principalities.

Jesus bled so we could have victory over disease, sickness, death, sin, and every devil, power and principality. His blood was shed for us. When we fully understand Christ's great sacrifice, we will be compelled to say, "Thank you Jesus for Your shed blood!" Then, as we think of Calvary's cross, we remember the redemptive blood of

Jesus given to us. We remember the price He paid. We remember the sacrifice. We remember the blessings of the Covenant and the blessings of redemption. We remember and even talk about the blessings bought for us with His blood.

So, we need to ask ourselves this: If the blood of Jesus is as precious as we say it is, and if it was by His blood that they overcame, why aren't we modern-day Christians doing anything in prayer to apply the power and the blessings of the blood of Jesus in our lives?

THE BLOOD IS ALIVE TODAY

The blood of Jesus is alive! Even though it fell to the ground 2000 years ago, it has not dried up.

Although long since evaporated, those pools of living blood on the ground at Golgotha still team with life and vitality the same life and vitality that coursed through the Master's veins so long ago. Where did the blood go?

But Christ came as High Priest of the good things to come, with the greater and more perfect tabernacle not made with hands, that is, not of this creation. Not with the blood of goats and calves, but with His own blood He entered the Most Holy Place once and for all, having obtained eternal redemption.

Hebrews 9:11, 12 But Christ being come an high priest of good things to come, by a greater and more perfect tabernacle, not made with hands, that is to say, not of this building; Neither by the blood of goats and calves, but by his own blood he entered in once into the holy place, having obtained eternal redemption *for us.*

His blood went to Heaven, into the Most Holy Place.

When He ascended and entered the Most Holy Place, Jesus presented His bloody, marred, beaten, battered body before the throne of His Father. He took that deformed and bruised body right into Heaven and showed it to the Father. It was not the shed blood of animals under the Old Covenant, but His own blood that poured out of His body and to the feet of the Father. His own blood covered the Throne Room of Heaven.

Essentially the scene was like this: Is it enough, Father? I am satisfied. The wages of sin is death, paid in full. And the gavel hit the stand and God's wrath was satisfied. Christ's blood made the way for us to enter into the Most Holy Place because of the power it had to forgive us of our sins and cleanse us. I am confident that when we arrive in Heaven we will see His blood. One day we will be absent from the body and present with the Lord. Together with Him, we will look on scenes of Calvary and see the blood in Heaven with our own eyes. The blood was the price of sin and is too precious to the Father for Him to allow it to dry up. That 2000 year-old blood in Heaven is as alive now as it was then.

THE BLOOD SPEAKS

Do you remember the blood of Abel? The Bible says that the blood of Abel cried out to God; it cried against sin and injustice. It demanded a price and it demanded justice. The blood of Abel cried of murder, sin, and the wickedness of man. It cried for atonement, justice, and righteousness.

Genesis 4:10 And he said, What hast thou done? the voice of thy brother's blood crieth unto me from the ground.

The blood of Jesus also speaks. It speaks of better things than that of Abel! "To Jesus the Mediator of the new covenant and to the blood of sprinkling that speaks better things than that of Abel."

Hebrews 12:24 And to Jesus the mediator of the new covenant, and to the blood of sprinkling, that speaketh better things than *that of* Abel.

Oh how wonderful and profound is the message of the blood of Christ! Do you know what the blood of Jesus says to us? "Justified, forgiven, paid-in-full, freed from sickness and disease. Demonic principalities and powers are disarmed. You can be near to Father God and experience His manifest glory. The way into the Most Holy Place is open. Come boldly before the throne of grace and worship My Father."

The blood of Jesus speaks with the same vitality, the same life, and the same power as it did when it first poured out of His body 2000 years ago! Man that blood is just as alive and scary to the devil today as it was the day Jesus died and took the keys of HELL and death right out of the devil's hand. The devil saw the blood and knew what it meant: "Paid-in-full and justified." Jesus was taking away his power, stripping him of his kingdom, and giving it back to man. Satan knew that we could now have dominion over him, over sickness and disease, that we could now advance the kingdom of God, and that we could experience again what Adam and Eve experienced in the Garden with the Father.

APPLY THE BLOOD

The blood of Jesus speaks, oh yes, but there is even more to the blood. We can apply it to our circumstances and to every area of our lives. Examine the account of the Passover in Exodus chapter 12. The Passover lamb foreshadowed Jesus. The events of the Passover night are the Old Testament foreshadowing of the salvation bought for us with Christ's blood. The Israelites took a lamb, killed it, and then sacrificed it. Afterward, they applied its blood to the doorposts of their homes so that when the angel of death came, it would "pass over" them. God would not allow harm to strike those of His people who were covered by the blood.

Just as the Israelites applied the blood of the sacrificed lamb to the doorposts of their homes, we can take the blood of the Lamb of God who was slain for the sin of the world and apply His blood to our lives. Because of the shed blood of Jesus the Lamb, we have eternal life the keys of life and death, and because of His broken body, the keys of healing and deliverance.

In the Old Testament, Moses, Aaron, and Aaron's sons used the sacrificial blood to anoint the tabernacle and everything in it, including the utensils, water basins, and garments. Aaron and his sons were anointed with it, and they poured out and sprinkled the blood of the lamb seven times around the altar as atonement for the sins of the people. As New Testament believers, because the living, powerful, and vital blood of Jesus was shed for each of us in intercession, we can reach right into

Heaven for it and apply it to circumstances. Through prayer and by faith you can also reach for the blood and anoint or apply it to everything in your life, including your spouse, children, job, your home, and everything in it.

The blood is available today to give us power to overcome. Thank God for the shed blood of Jesus in my life. In prayer, plead the blood of Jesus, that same blood that was brought before His throne, that same blood that was shed for the remission of your sin, and apply it to your life.

Reach into Heaven for the blood and use it for victory, saying, "I thank You Lord for it and I ask You to release it over my circumstances today." Say, "Satan! The blood of

Jesus is against you!" Then declare, "Father, I take of the shed blood and I apply its power against the devil in Jesus' name."

ANOINTING OF THE BLOOD

Do you know how to use the blood of Jesus? Remember, the blood of Jesus speaks. Speak the reality of what the blood of Jesus has done for you in your circumstances. Use the blood as a weapon by speaking against sicknesses. Speak of it against those devils. Make it known to demonic powers and principalities in the Heavenlies that you are armed and powerful with the shed blood of Jesus. The devil needs to know that you know what you have because of the redemptive covenant that God made with you on the cross at Calvary. Here is something interesting. In the consecration of the priests and the altar in the tabernacle, God's instructions to Moses were that they take some of the ram's blood and place it on the lobe of Aaron's right ear and onto the lobes of his son's right ears. Then He said to place more of the blood on the thumbs of their right hands and on the toes of their right feet. Finally, he instructed them to sprinkle the remaining blood on the altar.

Exodus 29:19-21 And thou shalt take the other ram; and Aaron and his sons shall put their hands upon the head of the ram. Then shalt thou kill the ram, and take of his blood, and put *it* upon the tip of the right ear of Aaron, and upon the tip of the right ear of his sons, and upon the thumb of their right hand, and upon the great toe of their right foot, and sprinkle the blood upon the altar round about. And thou shalt take of the blood that *is* upon the altar, and of the anointing oil, and sprinkle *it* upon Aaron, and upon his garments, and upon his sons, and upon the garments of his sons with him: and he shall be hallowed, and his garments, and his sons, and his sons' garments with him.

To be consecrated to God is to have His blood on you! Blood on your ear: Whom do you listen to? Blood on your thumb: Whom do you labor for? Blood on your big toe: Whom do you walk for, whose path are you on?

The blood was applied to hearing, to actions, to the walk. Consecration in those days lasted about seven days. Imagine spending an entire week washed with blood and yet in God's home (His tabernacle) in fellowship with Him.

Hebrews 9:14 How much more shall the blood of Christ, who through the eternal Spirit offered himself without spot to God, purge your conscience from dead works to serve the living God?

God also told Moses to take some of the blood that was on the altar and some of the anointing oil and to sprinkle it on Aaron and his garments, on Aaron's sons, and on their garments. When we learn to speak, apply, and employ the weapon of the power of the blood of Jesus in all we do and say and hear and walk, guess what happens? The anointing! The oil symbolizes the anointing, and oil always comes after the blood. Do you want an increase of the anointing? Preach the blood. Read it, speak it, and thank God for it! Remember what it has done for you. The blood is powerful! Lay hold of its power and then watch as the Holy Spirit arrives with the oil!

The Holy Ghost always honors Calvary. He confirms and honors the Gospel, for it is Calvary and repentance. The Gospel is forgiveness of sin, salvation, healing, and deliverance. Do you know why the Holy Ghost so loves the blood? Because the Bible says that Jesus offered Himself up once and for all through the eternal Spirit. It was through the power of the Holy Spirit that He offered His life as a sacrifice on the cross at Calvary. It was through the Holy Spirit that He offered Himself without spot to God. Rest assured that whenever you talk about that night, the Holy Ghost will show up with a powerful anointing. Most Importantly, Thank Him for the Blood Why not thank God right now for the blood. Come on! Thank Him for His shed blood at Calvary. Honor His blood.

Speak and apply it into your circumstances and thank Him that He is the Lamb of God who has taken away the sin of the world. Decree, in Jesus' name, that because of the shed blood, every devil departs from your home, and every sickness and infirmity breaks under the revelation of the power of the blood of Jesus. Declare that the power of Jesus' blood breaks the power and grip of death.

Ask for a sprinkling of the blood, the blood that defeats devils and principalities, the blood that destroys darkness and sin, the blood that overcomes death. Ask Him to wash away your sin and to cover you with His precious blood. Thank Him for triumph right now in every circumstance of your life. Thank Him for triumph over every demonic assignment, bondage, sin, and disease. You are blood-bought, blood-washed, and blood-freed! Thank Him for what His blood has bought for you. Now get ready for the Holy Spirit to come with fresh oil, a new and exciting anointing.

Ask God for the anointing that breaks the yoke of bondage and of slavery and receive the power of the blood of Jesus as He pours out the oil of freedom and blessings on you! Thanks be to God who always causes us to triumph in the name of Jesus. You can live as an overcomer and overcome the enemy. It was in God's plan all along.

Evangelism of Power

God is calling the Church to walk in power. A church without walls sharing the gospel is what God is speaking. This is what we need to reach the lost.

We need to set up tents and give prophetic words over the lost, while others gather the lost in the malls. We need anointed people to pray for the sick and minister to the hurting.

PROPHETIC EVANGELISM

1 Corinthians 14:23-26 If therefore the whole church be come together into one place, and all speak with tongues, and there

come in *those that are* unlearned, or unbelievers, will they not say that ye are mad? But if all prophesy, and there come in one that believeth not, or *one* unlearned, he is convinced of all, he is judged of all: And thus are the secrets of his heart made manifest; and so falling down on *his* face he will worship God, and report that God is in you of a truth. How is it then, brethren? when ye come together, every one of you hath a psalm, hath a doctrine, hath a tongue, hath a revelation, hath an interpretation. Let all things be done unto edifying.

PROPHETIC ACTIVATION

After training equipping and teaching on the prophetic, how to hear God's voice and prophesy. I activate and release to all to prophesy! They all prophesy over one another, if it can work in the church, Why not in the market place?

1 Corinthians 14:30, 31 If *any thing* be revealed to another that sitteth by, let the first hold his peace. For ye may all prophesy one by one, that all may learn, and all may be comforted.

Psalms 139:17, 18 How precious also are thy thoughts unto me, O God! how great is the sum of them! *If* I should count them, they are more in number than the sand: when I awake, I am still with thee.

You may just have a mental picture, in a restaurant practicing the word of knowledge. Ask God to show you something about the waitress.

We cannot operate in the gifts of the spirit in the market place because we turn off the gift and pressing in for the word outside the four walls of the church. We need an increased prophetic awareness. Let's start asking God for words when in unusual places, especially restaurants.

SAMARITAN AT THE WELL ANOINTING

God wants us to make ourselves available to him. Ask where he wants us to go and go! It's time for the Samaritan anointing. Jesus shared with this gentile woman in John chapter 4 a word of knowledge about her many husbands and the result was "Come, see a Man who told me all things that I ever did. Could this be the Christ? Then they went out of the city and came to Him. The whole city came because one woman received a word from God. God can use anybody.

POWER EVANGELISM STRATEGIES

1. Prophetic booths, market places, flea markets, mall or coffee shops and juice bars are great places.

2. Dream interpretation booths. (Remember we need to draw the lost. Sometimes you might be in places you need to give the language the people understand.)

3. Free prayer booths.

4. God is going to anoint street preaching again, like in the old time revivals.

5. Servant evangelism-- love acts carry power! Let's make ourselves available to God in a new way. Take it to the markets. Jesus had some of his greatest miracles and healings in the market. Mowing people's lawns showing the love of God.

Power for Deliverance

Deliverance is needed for the Body of Christ. If want to walk in power there will be a major need of deliverance power. This is a topic many within the Church today avoid. There is true deliverance we need and are to flow in.

The Dumb Man

Matthew 9:32, 33 As they went out, behold, they brought to him a dumb man possessed with a devil. And when the devil was cast out, the dumb spake: and the multitudes marvelled, saying, It was never so seen in Israel.

The Blind & Dumb Man

Matthew 12:22 Then was brought unto him one possessed with a devil, blind, and dumb: and he healed him, insomuch that the blind and dumb both spake and saw.

The Daughter

Matthew 15:22-28 And, behold, a woman of Canaan came out of the same coasts, and cried unto him, saying, Have mercy on me, O Lord, *thou* Son of David; my daughter is grievously vexed with a devil. But he answered her not a word. And his disciples came and besought him, saying, Send her away; for she crieth after us. But he answered and said, I am not sent but unto the lost sheep of the house of Israel. Then came she and worshipped him, saying, Lord, help me. But he answered and said, It is not meet to take the children's bread, and to cast *it* to dogs. And she said, Truth, Lord: yet the dogs eat of the crumbs which fall from their masters' table. Then Jesus answered and said unto her, O woman, great *is* thy faith: be it unto thee even as thou wilt. And her daughter was made whole from that very hour.

A Lunatic Child

Matthew 17:14-18 And when they were come to the multitude, there came to him a *certain* man, kneeling down to him, and saying, Lord, have mercy on my son: for he is lunatick, and sore vexed: for ofttimes he falleth into the fire, and oft into the water. And I brought him to thy disciples, and they could not cure him. Then Jesus answered and said, O faithless and perverse generation, how long shall I be with you? how long shall I suffer you? bring him hither to me. And Jesus rebuked the devil; and he departed out of him: and the child was cured from that very hour.

The Man in the Synagogue

Mark 1:23-26 And there was in their synagogue a man with an unclean spirit; and he cried out, Saying, Let *us* alone; what have we to do with thee, thou Jesus of Nazareth? art thou come to destroy us? I know thee who thou art, the

Holy One of God. And Jesus rebuked him, saying, Hold thy peace, and come out of him. And when the unclean spirit had torn him, and cried with a loud voice, he came out of him.

Mary Magdalene

Mark 16:9 Now when *Jesus* was risen early the first *day* of the week, he appeared first to Mary Magdalene, out of whom he had cast seven devils.

Jesus

Matthew 4:24 And his fame went throughout all Syria: and they brought unto him all sick people that were taken with divers diseases and torments, and those which were possessed with devils, and those which were lunatick, and those that had the palsy; and he healed them.

Matthew 8:16 When the even was come, they brought unto him many that were possessed with devils: and he cast out the spirits with *his* word, and healed all that were sick:

Mark 3:22 And the scribes which came down from Jerusalem said, He hath Beelzebub, and by the prince of the devils casteth he out devils.

Luke 4:41 And devils also came out of many, crying out, and saying, Thou art Christ the Son of God. And he rebuking *them* suffered them not to speak: for they knew that he was Christ.

Power over devils given to the disciples

Matthew 10:1 And when he had called unto *him* his twelve disciples, he gave them power *against* unclean spirits, to cast them out, and to heal all manner of sickness and all manner of disease.

Mark 6:7 And he called *unto him* the twelve, and began to send them forth by two and two; and gave them power over unclean spirits;

Mark 16:17 And these signs shall follow them that believe; In my name shall they cast out devils; they shall speak with new tongues;

Disciples casting out devils

Luke 10:17 And the seventy returned again with joy, saying, Lord, even the devils are subject unto us through thy name.

Peter

Acts 5:16 There came also a multitude *out* of the cities round about unto Jerusalem, bringing sick folks, and them which were vexed with unclean spirits: and they were healed every one.
(healed everyone includes the casting out devils.)

Paul

Acts 16:16-18 And it came to pass, as we went to prayer, a certain damsel possessed with a spirit of divination met us, which brought her masters much gain by soothsaying: The same followed Paul and us, and cried, saying, These men are the servants of the most high God, which shew unto us the way of salvation. And this did she many days. But Paul, being grieved, turned and said to the spirit, I command thee in the name of Jesus Christ to come out of her. And he came out the same hour.

Acts 19:12 So that from his body were brought unto the sick handkerchiefs or aprons, and the diseases departed from them, and the evil spirits went out of them.

Ordinary Man Casting Out Devils

Mark 9:38 And John answered him, saying, Master, we saw one

casting out devils in thy name, and he followeth not us: and we forbad him, because he followeth not us.

Phillip

Acts 8:7 For unclean spirits, crying with loud voice, came out of many that were possessed *with them:* and many taken with palsies, and that were lame, were healed.

The disciples could not cast out

Mark 9:18 And wheresoever he taketh him, he teareth him: and he foameth, and gnasheth with his teeth, and pineth away: and I spake to thy disciples that they should cast him out; and they could not.

Mark 9:28 And when he was come into the house, his disciples asked him privately, Why could not we cast him out?

The exercise

Acts 19:13-17 Then certain of the vagabond Jews, exorcists, took upon them to call over them which had evil spirits the name of the Lord Jesus, saying, We adjure you by Jesus whom Paul preacheth. And there were seven sons of *one* Sceva, a Jew, *and* chief of the priests, which did so. And the evil spirit answered and said, Jesus I know, and Paul I know; but who are ye? And the man in whom the evil spirit was leaped on them, and overcame them, and prevailed against them, so that they fled out of that house naked and wounded. And this was known to all the Jews and Greeks also dwelling at

Ephesus; and fear fell on them all, and the name of the Lord Jesus was magnified.

The Man Possessed

Matthew 12:43-45 When the unclean spirit is gone out of a man, he walketh through dry places, seeking rest, and findeth none. Then he saith, I will return into my house from whence I came out; and when he is come, he findeth *it* empty, swept, and garnished. Then goeth he, and taketh with himself seven other spirits more wicked than himself, and they enter in and dwell there: and the last *state* of that man is worse than the first. Even so shall it be also unto this wicked generation.

Testify of Jesus

Matthew 8:29 And, behold, they cried out, saying, What have we to do with thee, Jesus, thou Son of God? art thou come hither to torment us before the time?

Mark 1:23, 24 And there was in their synagogue a man with an unclean spirit; and he cried out, Saying, Let *us* alone; what have we to do with thee, thou Jesus of Nazareth? art thou come to destroy us? I know thee who thou art, the Holy One of God.

Believe and tremble (even the devils believe)

James 2:19 Thou believest that there is one God; thou doest well: the devils also believe, and tremble.

(A saying I have used before the devil is more faithful than most saints.)

Punishment

Matthew 25:41 Then shall he say also unto them on the left hand, Depart from me, ye cursed, into everlasting fire, prepared for the devil and his angels:

2 Peter 2:4 For if God spared not the angels that sinned, but cast *them* down to hell, and delivered *them* into chains of darkness, to be reserved unto judgment;

Revelations 12:7-9 And there was war in heaven: Michael and his angels fought against the dragon; and the dragon fought and his angels, And prevailed not; neither was their place found any more in heaven. And the great dragon was cast out, that old serpent, called the Devil, and Satan, which deceiveth the whole world: he was cast out into the earth, and his angels were cast out with him.

John 5:17-19 But Jesus answered them, My Father worketh hitherto, and I work. Therefore the Jews sought the more to kill him, because he not only had broken the sabbath, but said also that God was his Father, making himself equal with God. Then answered Jesus and said unto them, Verily, verily, I say unto you, The Son can do nothing of himself, but what he seeth the Father do: for what things soever he doeth, these also doeth the Son likewise.

Acts 10:38 How God anointed Jesus of Nazareth with the Holy Ghost and with power: who went about doing good, and healing all that were oppressed of the devil; for God was with him.

Matthew 28:18 And Jesus came and spake unto them, saying, All power is given unto me in heaven and in earth.

Philippians 4:13 I can do all things through Christ which strengtheneth me.

Reign for Resurrection

There is a higher level the Church is to reign with greater power. There is power of resurrection coming to those who reign with Him. In this Chapter I will establish the connection between reigning and resurrection with a very convincing description of the power and authority that is ours when we enter the kingdom of Jesus by being born of the Spirit. Taking his water baptism as an example, I'll share how that prophetic act marked him for life; and you'll be quickened with excitement as you discover how the same glory that raised Christ from the dead is available to work in you too. You'll also learn what it takes to receive your full inheritance, and about how resurrection goes hand in hand with reigning and advancing God's kingdom NOW.

Then I will give more keys for reigning and resurrection that connect to the importance of walking by faith.

We don't need resurrection power in heaven; no one is going to be raised from the dead in heaven! But we certainly need the anointing to flow out of our lives here on earth. I mean the anointing that gives life it's essential if we're going to partner with God to overthrow the powers of darkness because both death and destruction stalk the earth continually. That anointing will empower us to walk full out in our authority reigning being determined believers who advance God's kingdom in the earth, just like it is in heaven. The stakes are high, but resurrection power will make the difference! Now, you might be wondering how "resurrection power" and "reigning" work together and how both can be activated in your life. To answer that, we'll examine several essential elements in this Chapter, real keys for reigning and walking in resurrection power.

THE NEW BIRTH OPENS GOD'S KINGDOM!

First of all, let's acknowledge together that God is a God of order. Just try and imagine what the world would be like if He wasn't! He is orderly, and it's by His design that our first nature is spirit. Yes we have a body but the spirit comes first. He created us that way.

Now, think for a few moments about your first nature, spirit, in the context of your born again experience. Your new birth was momentous! Because everything about you today, in Christ, hinges on that experience! That's when your spirit came to life alive in Christ.

1 Peter 3:18 For Christ also hath once suffered for sins, the just for the unjust, that he might bring us to God, being put to death in the flesh, but quickened by the Spirit:

You are no longer a natural being that has a spirit; you're a spiritual being that has a body!
You're a brand new creation in Christ who lives, for a time, on the earth; one who is learning to live in

your true nature, in Christ Jesus, which is spirit.

2 Corinthians 5:17 Therefore if any man *be* in Christ, *he is* a new creature: old things are passed away; behold, all things are become new.

The fact is, (for all true believers), the moment we're born again an earth shaking shift takes place. We are transported from the kingdom of darkness into the kingdom of God's beloved Son! As well, we come into the right position for receiving God's great benefits, which include the necessary keys for activating our spiritual senses. So, you can see that the new birth opens up God's kingdom. However, if you don't have the new birth, then you certainly won't be seeing or entering His kingdom!

John 3:3-5 Jesus answered and said unto him, Verily, verily, I say unto thee, Except a man be born again, he cannot see the kingdom of God. Nicodemus saith unto him, How can a man be born when he is old? can he enter the second time into his mother's womb, and be born? Jesus answered, Verily, verily, I say unto thee, Except a man be born of water and *of* the Spirit, he cannot enter into the kingdom of God.

Yes, we have a body but we're spiritual beings first, and though we're here on earth, our citizenship is actually in heaven.

Philippians 3:20 For our conversation is in heaven; from whence also we look for the Saviour, the Lord Jesus Christ:

I'm a citizen of heaven first, and I'm a Canadian citizen. Keeping that revelation in mind, did you know that you and I don't have to wait to die and go to heaven for heaven to be a reality in our lives? I say that because God's word says that "the kingdom of God is at hand" it's a "now" word and "the kingdom of God is within you."

Mark 1:15 And saying, The time is fulfilled, and the kingdom of God is at hand: repent ye, and believe the gospel.

Luke 17:21 Neither shall they say, Lo here! or, lo there! for, behold, the kingdom of God is within you.

Colossians 1:27 To whom God would make known what *is* the riches of the glory of this mystery among the Gentiles; which is Christ in you, the hope of glory:

LIVE IN CHRIST, DIE TO SELF & EXPERIENCE YOUR RESURRECTION!

Ironically, soon after the new birth, a death experience comes along death to self, death to our carnal nature that "old man!" But we can thank God for the resurrection that follows! One way to illustrate this whole paradox is by sharing about my water baptism. I was told, "Bill, something is going to happen when you go down in that water;

you're going to come up a new man!" It was true. At the convergence of two acts something happened.

Here's how:

First, when I went under the water, I identified with Christ when He died and was placed into a tomb; I was dying to self. In other words, when you're baptized you identify with the truth, and that truth is that you have died to your old nature; its sins and passions you've died. Believe it! "Or do you not know that as many of us as were baptized into Christ Jesus were baptized into His death?

Romans 6:3 Know ye not, that so many of us as were baptized into Jesus Christ were baptized into his death?

It's done!

Second, when I came up out of the water, just as Christ was resurrected, so was I! Resurrection into newness of life!

Romans 6:4 Therefore we are buried with him by baptism into death: that like as Christ was raised up from the dead by the glory of the Father, even so we also should walk in newness of life.

Done! A spiritual impartation happened; it was activated by the power of what was taking place in the spirit by that prophetic act.

Although we tend to put resurrection in the future, it isn't just a future event! And when that revelation hit me I started developing a resurrection mindset, thinking: My spirit has been raised from the dead. I know what it's like, that same "glory" that raised Christ from the dead. That same glory is what touched my spirit and made me alive! I've already experienced the very same resurrection power that raised Jesus up from the tomb; it not only has touched me, it's working inside of me! It's the anointing, the Holy Spirit that dwells in me! That revelation was like being gloriously born again, again!

SO WHAT DOES RESURRECTION LOOK LIKE?

I'm talking about the likeness of His resurrection and the idea that as we walk in "newness of life" we walk in victory.

You can't tell me that there is resurrection power and ruling operating in your life if you're being defeated in your own spirit. That resurrection power is yours if you'll use it! At your disposal is the Spirit of God. He is the Spirit of holiness, which is the Spirit of resurrection, and only He can make death die; only the Holy Spirit can help us to overcome what the flesh wants. He responds when we seek holiness and demonstrate reverential fear of the Lord.

Actually, the Spirit of holiness is seven things. The Holy Spirit: corrects, counsels, strengthens, helps, intercedes, is our defense attorney and the comforter called alongside. It's the Holy Spirit residing within us, and the effective working of His power working within us, that makes us holy, that sanctifies us, and makes us righteous. Two keys are: His grace and our obedience. We can't say that we're holy without obedience. In fact, we can only manifest God's kingdom to the extent we're willing to sacrifice, surrender and be obedient. The greater the obedience and total surrender, the greater the manifestation of power, and the model is Jesus.

With resurrection power, our old self becomes so dead that we become dead to the things that the flesh wants. It's newness of life, which means: overcoming sickness, disease and poverty; reigning in resurrection; raising the dead. What a rich inheritance! And it's ours today! Not just when we get to heaven.

FIRST INTIMACY, THEN INHERITANCE ON EARTH & IN HEAVEN

Just look at what the Apostle Paul said in his prayer to the Ephesian church about our inheritance:

Ephesians 1:11 In whom also we have obtained an inheritance, being predestinated according to the purpose of him who worketh all things after the counsel of his own will:

He goes on to describe three aspects in our inheritance: that we may know one, what is the hope of His calling; two, what are the riches of the glory of His inheritance in the saints; and three, what is the exceeding greatness of His power toward us who believe according to the working of His mighty power which He worked in Christ when He raised Him from the dead and seated Him at His right hand in the heavenly places.

Ephesians 1:17-20 That the God of our Lord Jesus Christ, the Father of glory, may give unto you the spirit of wisdom and revelation in the knowledge of him: The eyes of your understanding being enlightened; that ye may know what is the hope of his calling, and what the riches of the glory of his inheritance in the saints, And what *is* the exceeding greatness of his power to us-ward who believe, according to the working of his mighty power, Which he wrought in Christ, when he raised him from the dead, and set *him* at his own right hand in the heavenly *places,*

So, I'm not just focused on who I am in Christ, I'm focused on discovering who Christ is in me.

In that discovery, I'm being drawn into a deep friendship with God in the secret place. That's where I'm finding out more and more about the scope of my inheritance for instance, reigning and resurrection power, and more. On the other hand, if I was continually ignoring the Holy Spirit, even though I am born again and God's word says I can enter the kingdom of God, I would not be in the right position to receive all of my inheritance. Think about this. We can enter the kingdom of God, yes, but not everyone that enters the kingdom of God inherits the kingdom of God! The key to inheritance is intimacy and revelation and through this I know that, spiritually, I've been made a "king". This is my spiritual status, to reign on this earth and so I'm beginning to reign today! But, of course, without intimacy with God, I won't have the reigning and resurrection power! What we gain as we advance and grow here, we take with us into eternity. Don't miss this.

The degree to which we faithfully act on the revelation God gives us, is the degree of responsibility that we will have in eternity. There are degrees; and this will affect our "brightness" in heaven. Every star differs in glory. We're mistaken if we think that if we all ended up in heaven right now, we'd be equals; that somehow once we enter the pearly gates everything that I see, you see; and everything that becomes my experience, becomes your experience. Or that whatever we've done here doesn't count.

I, for one, want to get to know God; I want to rule and reign in the universe and hang out with the angels. "God, can you create another planet with souls on it that need to be saved and send me there?" I want to talk about different things with Michael (archangel) and Gabriel (angel). "Come on Abraham! We've got to have a conversation about" Heaven would be pretty boring if we just kind of showed up and said, "Here I am! Done!"

Reigning and resurrection certainly goes hand in hand with understanding the scope of our inheritance in Christ in the light of both the here and now, and eternity. Not only do we reign in eternity, we are meant to reign here on earth now. Resurrection is about reigning in life, having dominion, taking authority, advancing the kingdom, and destroying the works of the devil NOW!

Get ready for this new level then you'll be ready to receive two great keys for defeating whatever death brings as I release about the connection between sin and death and how death no longer has dominion. As well, since strong, vibrant faith is essential for reigning and resurrection power, I'll focus on faith and how to protect what you believe. At the close of this teaching I will take a look at the miraculous virtue of Jesus Christ. Be blessed as you grow in the spiritual stature that God has for you!

In God's kingdom there is just so much to look forward to! In fact, God will take us as far as we want to go. I'm talking about depth, the deep things of God.

And yet, as I've been thinking about how the whole concept of resurrection is perceived by many in the church, it's like a lot of believers only see its relevance in light of a Resurrection Sunday sermon. Or others think that resurrection is all about our heavenly bodies, the rapture, or the second coming it tends to be something in the future.

RESURRECTION IS ACTUALLY AN ELEMENTARY PRINCIPLE

On top of that, some Christians consider the whole idea about resurrection, or the opportunity to actually raise the dead, to be pretty radical. But according to scripture, resurrection from the dead is part of the foundation of Christian belief. It's actually an elementary principle!

Hebrews 6:1, 2 Therefore leaving the principles of the doctrine of Christ, let us go on unto perfection; not laying again the foundation of repentance from dead works, and of faith toward God, Of the doctrine of baptisms, and of laying on of hands, and of resurrection of the dead, and of eternal judgment. Still, even though resurrection from the dead is a foundational principle, in order to actually receive and walk in all the benefits involved in what resurrection promises, we need to have our minds renewed.

DEATH NO LONGER HAS DOMINION

I shared about how I was developing a "resurrection mindset" and how I realized that the same glory (or resurrection power) that raised Jesus up after his crucifixion had not only touched me; it was working inside of me. Let me explain another aspect concerning this revelation; my point being today, I've come to understand that "death no longer has dominion."

Romans 6:9 Knowing that Christ being raised from the dead dieth no more; death hath no more dominion over him.

Now, because I am a born again believer and I believe that death no longer has dominion, and since sickness and disease cause death, then I have the right to refuse the diseases of the world, the viruses, the sicknesses, the bacteria or whatever exists in the world that brings death. I refuse it!

Now, I don't deny the circumstances; I mean if you have cancer, or a tumor, it's real. But there is something about when your body begins to understand that your spirit is raised from the dead "But if the Spirit of Him who raised Jesus from the dead dwells in you, He who raised Christ Jesus from the dead will also give life to your mortal bodies through His Spirit who dwells in you." Cancer! You can't live here!

The same goes for poverty. Poverty is death. Any kind of oppression in your life, any kind of torment, any kind of depression it's the work of the devil and it is defeated because death no longer has dominion! In fact, death has to bow! It bowed to Jesus wherever He went. Can you imagine how tense darkness became every time Jesus showed up on the scene?

The Lord would show up and devils would start screaming. And the dead were raised!

Mark 5:7 And cried with a loud voice, and said, What have I to do with thee, Jesus, *thou* Son of the most high God? I adjure thee by God, that thou torment me not.

John 11:38-44 Jesus therefore again groaning in himself cometh to the grave. It was a cave, and a stone lay upon it. Jesus said, Take ye away the stone. Martha, the sister of him that was dead, saith unto him, Lord, by this time he stinketh: for he hath been *dead* four days. Jesus saith unto her, Said I not unto thee, that, if thou wouldest believe, thou shouldest see the glory of God? Then they took away the stone *from the place* where the dead was laid. And Jesus lifted up *his* eyes, and said, Father, I thank thee that thou hast heard me. And I knew that thou hearest me always: but because of the people which stand by I said *it,* that they may believe that thou hast sent me. And when he thus had spoken, he cried with a loud voice, Lazarus, come forth. And he that was dead came forth, bound hand and foot with graveclothes: and his face was bound about with a napkin. Jesus saith unto them, Loose him, and let him go.

Likewise, when believers know who they are in Christ, sickness and death must bow! For example, when I'm ministering in a crusade, I think like this: The death around me in this crusade isn't allowed to be at work here! Since death no longer has dominion, I take my God-given authority and make a decree; then whatever is of the "realm of death" has to bow to resurrection! There are times when I walk into a room and the diseases in people's bodies can only hold on until I cast out a (demonic) spirit with a word. "I see you, devil. Get out!"

DEATH IS ALWAYS ROOTED IN SIN

Romans 6:10, 11 For in that he died, he died unto sin once: but in that he liveth, he liveth unto God. Likewise reckon ye also yourselves to be dead indeed unto sin, but alive unto God through Jesus Christ our Lord.

So, count yourselves to be dead to sin in the same way that Jesus counted Himself dead and resurrected count yourselves dead and resurrected. That means death no longer has dominion over you!

Romans 6:12 Let not sin therefore reign in your mortal body, that ye should obey it in the lusts thereof.

Friends, there is a place where because we love Jesus, we obey His commands; and because there is a love, we don't want to wound His heart. After all, we're in a covenant relationship with Jesus Christ and we don't want to hurt the One we love. There is a choice if you let sin reign, then death reigns because the power of death is always rooted in sin especially willful, habitual sin, offense, bitterness, and unforgiveness.

In fact, it wasn't until one man sinned by disobeying God that sickness, poverty, bondage and death came into the world and spread to all mankind. Initially, Adam (and Eve) brought the curse, and it became the curse of the law.

Then every conceivable sin that you could imagine, every conceivable sickness or disease, came into the curse. But we were (and are) rescued from the curse because ultimately, Jesus Christ conquered death. Through His death and resurrection, our sin and death are defeated and now both freedom from sin and death can spread to all mankind!

1 Corinthians 15:22 For as in Adam all die, even so in Christ shall all be made alive.

1 Corinthians 15:45 And so it is written, The first man Adam was made a living soul; the last Adam *was made* a quickening spirit.

The law of the spirit of life in Christ Jesus has made me free from the law of sin and death.

Romans 8:2 For the law of the Spirit of life in Christ Jesus hath made me free from the law of sin and death.

There is a law! That law of sin and death is a spiritual law and all of hell is ready to back-up that law.

But the law of the Spirit of life, the law of resurrection in Christ Jesus, has made me free from the law of sin and death and all of heaven is ready to enforce that law!

Therefore, the truth is, it's a law that I'm not sick (sickness can be defeated)! It's a law that I'm the blessed one. It's a spiritual law: "Devil you can't hold me down!" There is a law of the spirit realm, the law of the spirit world, the law of resurrection!

But, in order to ensure your freedom from the curse of the law, don't miss these three vital principles: First, remember, the law of sin and death can only be broken by Jesus Christ and if you're born again. Second, God can only enforce the law of the spirit of life in Christ Jesus as you do your part by confessing your sins and asking Him to forgive you and cleanse you.

1 John 1:9 If we confess our sins, he is faithful and just to forgive us

our sins, and to cleanse us from all unrighteousness.

Third, you must also take responsibility for using your authority against the enemy's attacks, but you can only do a thorough job if you know who you are in Christ. Then the ruler of this world (the devil) has nothing to hang on to, no claim on you. After all, Satan couldn't do a thing to stop anything Jesus did! Why? It was because Jesus was without sin the ruler of this world is coming, and he has nothing in Me. That's what I'm aiming for! How about you?

John 14:30 Hereafter I will not talk much with you: for the prince of this world cometh, and hath nothing in me.

As I said, only the Holy Spirit, the Spirit of holiness can help us conquer what the flesh wants. True overcoming only happens as we abide in Christ, not having our own righteousness "which is from the law, but that which is through faith in Christ, the righteousness which is from God by faith."

Philippians 3:9, 10 And be found in him, not having mine own righteousness, which is of the law, but that which is through the faith of Christ, the righteousness which is of God by faith: That I may know him, and the power of his resurrection, and the fellowship of his sufferings, being made conformable unto his death;

You can't even get to the power of His resurrection until you can say, "I know Him!" There will be no power of Christ's resurrection working in your life unless you know Him intimately. It's about intimacy, but not just an intimacy wherein you spend time with the Lord. I'm talking about being "one in the spirit." Then God's glory is sure to shine through you and the people around you will notice this,

Acts 4:13 Now when they saw the boldness of Peter and John, and perceived that they were unlearned and ignorant men, they marvelled; and they took knowledge of them, that they had been with Jesus.

Friends, when you've "been with Jesus" like Peter and John you'll know what real faith is.

REAL FAITH BRINGS REIGNING AND RESURRECTION POWER

Look at what Paul the apostle said about faith:

Galatians 2:20 I am crucified with Christ: nevertheless I live; yet not I, but Christ liveth in me: and the life which I now live in the flesh I live by the faith of the Son of God, who loved me, and gave himself for me.

It bears repeating: "the life that I now live, I live by faith." You see, you're not going to have resurrection without faith. We must understand what faith, real faith is and how faith works! As a matter of fact, get every book, get every series that you can on faith!

Equally, always remember that faith and intimacy go hand in hand. Just as I said in the beginning of this Chapter, if intimacy with God is lacking there will be no reigning and resurrection power, anointing will not manifest without you being full of faith.

TAKE STEPS TO PROTECT YOUR FAITH & PRESS IN ALL THE WAY

So we need to remove the unbelief. Actually, Jesus "removed unbelief" by having the people who were in fear and/or unbelief leave the location where He was about to perform a miracle.

Luke 8:51-55 And when he came into the house, he suffered no man to go in, save Peter, and James, and John, and the father and the mother of the maiden. And all wept, and bewailed her: but he said, Weep not; she is not dead, but sleepeth. And they laughed him to scorn, knowing that she was dead. And he put them all out, and took her by the hand, and called, saying, Maid, arise. And her spirit came again, and she arose straightway: and he commanded to give her meat.

Because there is something about being sure that those that are with you are just as "in faith" as you are. Unbelief hinders miracles. Jesus, Himself, was hindered from doing miracles in his hometown because of the people's unbelief. For instance, I've had meetings where I was full of faith, but other people there brought their unbelief into the meeting and their lack of faith hindered the flow. I've had to say on a few occasions, "If you don't believe and you're a skeptic, I want you to leave the meeting right now." Until they left, I could not move in the realm of miracles fully.

So protect your faith. Put boundaries in place to protect what you believe. Here is an example of what I mean by "boundaries." Sometimes there are certain influences it might be from the people around you who want to challenge your beliefs yet not in a positive way. But when you have worked through your Christian beliefs with good, sound, mature, men and women and, for instance, you believe that healing and prosperity are inherent in salvation; protect that belief. There are things that I won't even entertain because I don't want to mess up my groove. I won't even debate it. I don't want to be sidetracked or waste my time by allowing such things to get into my grid!

Faith is something you go after and you keep.

Hebrews 11:6 But without faith *it is* impossible to please *him:* for he that cometh to God must believe that he is, and *that* he is a rewarder of them that diligently seek him.

Contend and be aggressive about pressing in. The Bible says: "And from the time John the Baptist began preaching and baptizing until now, the Kingdom of Heaven has been forcefully advancing."

Matthew 11:12 And from the days of John the Baptist until now the kingdom of heaven suffereth violence, and the violent take it by force.

So keep warring, don't let up; be persistent like the widow. She just kept coming to the judge, asking for justice and in the end the Lord said, "Hear what the unjust judge said. And shall God not avenge His own elect who cry out day and night to Him, though He bears long with them? I tell you that He will avenge them speedily.

Nevertheless, when the Son of Man comes, will He really find faith on the earth?" Press in, contend and be aggressive like the Prophet Elijah, after he discerned that rain was coming. He went into intercession seven times on Mount Carmel, each time sending his servant to check and see if rain was on the way. So don't stop praying and believing mid-way. Pray through till you're convinced, based on what God already said and begin to walk in an attitude of thanksgiving even if your circumstances aren't changing. Remember, you're pressing in for what you know God wants you to have. Receive what He said, by faith; yes, acknowledge the circumstances, but at the same time, what you have received from God by faith is more real.

THROUGH FAITH IN THE WORKING OF GOD

Resurrection happens through faith in the working of God.

Colossians 2:12 Buried with him in baptism, wherein also ye are risen with *him* through the faith of the operation of God, who hath raised him from the dead.

There is a connection between understanding the effective working of His power, the power that works within you and me, and the outward power that manifests. An example would be when someone is healed in their body when the manifest power of God is evident in a meeting, but it works according to the connection between the manifest power, outward manifest kingdom power, and the power that works within you.

Also, instead of being so focused on getting more power, we need to focus more on having faith "through the working of God." We need to understand how the power that's on the inside works and begin to focus on strengthening the inner man, and learning how to tap into the anointing that we already have on the inside. So we need to build ourselves up and recharge the "dunamis power" of the "battery" that we already have on the inside.

And one way to build ourselves up in our most holy faith is to pray in tongues. We'll activate the "dunamis generator!" As we do, through faith and working with God, resurrection life and power will manifest! I don't want to close this series, without mentioning how the dunamis generator is directly connected to the virtue of Christ that's inside you and me "Christ in you." It's a river that works on the inside, 24 hours a day. It's like a generator, seven days a week.

The Power of Partnership

This has power when saints of God come in agreement for a purpose. As a result of a scriptural promise, I believe that Revival waves of glory, as a ministry, can tap into another level of authority to impact your life. When you partner with us, we can all come into agreement for powerful breakthroughs in your life, based on Philippians 1:3. This verse expresses our commitment to you: I thank my God in all my remembrance of you. And in every prayer of mine I always make mention and petition for you with all joy and delight? In Philippians 1, Paul the Apostle is speaking to his partners as if it's his partner's conference. Now I can honestly say as a ministry when we pray, and when I pray personally?

Not every prayer that we pray and not every day that I pray? But several times a week when we pray for you, we make petition for you like Paul. And not just for five minutes? We mean sometimes an entire hour or more we actually pray and cover, world wide, those that are a part of Revival Waves of Glory through prayer and financial partnership.

This doesn't mean that we don't appreciate each one who might be a guest or a friend that comes to the conferences and gives an offering to the Lord when they are blessed. Actually, we have supporters that follow us around the State of Illinois and Missouri. We thank God for them. They may even give more than an average monthly partner gives in the time that they're in our meetings. However, the partners we are talking about are the ones that do something each month to say, we are committed to what you are doing in God. It might be five dollars a month? But they have made that monthly commitment. We thank God for them just as much as we thank God for the ones that say, "here is $500." They drop it in the offering that one time at one conference.

Yeah, we have people like that and we appreciate them. But you know, there is something more powerful, I believe that God wants to build families.

Jesus had partners. In fact, in Jesus' traveling ministry, there were women and a few men that were ordained by God to minister to Jesus out of their substance. That was the call of God upon their life? They would travel with Jesus and to minister financially to the needs of Jesus and the disciples. Some of them were rich, prominent, business men and rich, prominent, business women. John the Baptist had his partners too. In fact, Today, as well, each ministry, whether Billy Graham's, Benny Hinn's or T.L. Osbourne's, has partners that God has specifically called to come along side. Many believers are also called to support unknown works in the inner city. As a ministry, Revival Waves of Glory is also called to support other ministries. We want to sow into what great ministries are going too. We want to sow into the lives of children, of orphans. We want to sow into mercy ministries and into the poor. Each of us needs to hear from the Lord where we need to give.

This is not about getting you to give; we are just talking about faith for the anointing that is going to come on your lives as we agree together in prayer for the blessing of the Lord on you. I also want you to have a biblical understanding that God does call people to minister out of their substance. That is what you're doing when we pray or partner financially. Whether you give $5 regularly or $25 or $500, God sees that as partnership. And so we want to appreciate the commitment of such partners.

So here is Paul talking to his partners saying, I am praying for you. Like Paul, I am also saying, I am praying for you. We have made a commitment to pray for you and to cover your families. Years ago, when God called me into the ministry He said, Today is the day that you are going to be in the ministry. Today is the day; I am calling you out. You are going into the nations today!? This call came after a profound visitation of God's spirit, hours a day for months. I had been having this overwhelming basking time in the Lord's presence and was just enjoying His glory.

You see, most people think preachers just want money. However, a lot of people in the church today don't understand the importance of partnering with a ministry. For example, God may have called you to the healing ministry and you want to participate in giving and receiving. The question is: What kind of receiving will it be? You may be wondering what I can offer you, because I am not giving you money. Well, think about the anointing that God has placed upon my life it's a healing prophetic and revelatory anointing. So what do you have a right to receive as you stand before God in faith? By partnering with us for the healing anointing to be sent to the world, you can receive a special healing anointing to come on your life to heal your body. What about the anointing you need to come upon your life to heal your kids and to heal your family? Then you can also believe to receive the anointing the Lord has placed upon my life for open heavens and prophetic revelation or the anointing that God has placed upon the ministry for humanitarian aid and mercy. When you partner with us through your giving, you are actually opening up a credit account.

You see, partnership is reciprocal. That's why we will have partner meetings, banquets and lunches with special times of ministry where we can say it's time for the partners to receive. We want to see the same anointing we carry into the nations come upon our partners.

Paul continues his discussion of partnership saying, for even in Thessalonica you sent me contributions for my needs, not only once but a second time. Not that I seek or am eager for (your) gift, but I do seek and am eager for the fruit which increases to your credit? (They are the) fragrant odors of an offering and sacrifice which God welcomes and in which He delights? (Phil. 4:16). Through this Chapter, we want to echo Paul's heart; we want to see that you are blessed, that a harvest of blessing accumulates to your account. He talks about gifts being a fragrant odor, an offering and a sacrifice which God welcomes and delights in. Then he says that because of their partnership, my God will liberally supply (fill to the full) your every need according to His riches in glory in Christ Jesus.

Most people don't understand that this verse, Philippians 4:19, is in the context of partnership. Many people in the church today claim the promise that God will supply all their needs. Yet Paul is saying, No, no, no. My God shall supply all your needs because of your partnership, because of your sowing, because you are on the front-lines when every person is saved, healed and delivered. We can only claim Philippians 4:19 when we are sowing or giving. Often we think of this sowing and reaping in the context of finances. But God wants to supply all your need. As you partner with us, and as you read this teaching, I want you to grow in faith for provision for your need. I want you to have faith for your children this morning because as you have helped me restore other families, God is going to restore your family. Isn't that tremendous?!

We need to understand that partnership is a covenant. It's an agreement between two parties. Let's see what the Lord said to Moses about his covenant partners: Count up the plunder that was taken of man and beast you and Eleazar the priest and the chief fathers of the congregation; and divide the plunder into two parts, between those who took part in the war, who went out to battle, and all the congregation (who stayed home)? (Numbers 31: 25). Just like Moses' warriors, when we obey the word of the Lord and risk our spiritual lives on the spiritual battlefields. Our partners at home share the rewards of those at war on the front lines.

At Revival Waves of Glory, we are praying that the anointing of God's Spirit will come on our partners. In scripture we can actually see several different anointings. The first few verses of Isaiah 61 actually list ten results of the anointings of God's Spirit in Jesus' life. The Spirit anointed Jesus for the purpose of preaching the good news, healing broken hearts, setting captives free, among other things. King David said he had been anointed with fresh oil; God wants to do the same for us.

The Lord also wants to release new oil in us a new manifestation of God's presence, power and gifts on our lives. Let's cry out: God I want the new oil!? Let's ask the Lord to recharge everything that we have and everything that we've done let it be fresh and new. How about new oil, a new mantle, a new anointing, a new gifting of God's spirit? David spoke of this new anointing: But my horn you have exalted like a wild ox; I have been anointed with fresh oil? (Psalms 92:10). Not only was David's anointing fresh, but it was an anointing of strength like that of an ox. The first thing that comes when the anointing comes upon your life is a divine impartation of that! It's the anointing of strength! I'm ready to be like the wild ox, to charge again. I'm ready to harvest again. I'm ready to plough again. All of us need that anointing of strength, especially ministers and pastors who have been in ministry for any amount of time, who have become tired and need a refreshing. You need to be anointed with fresh oil.

The anointing of God's Spirit brings everything that you need. In fact, it's in God's anointing that provision comes. So many people in the church today and so many ministries in the church today are trying to build without that anointing oil. Nobody would want to come to our meetings or want to be a partner if we didn't have any oil. As David said, My people will volunteer freely in the day of His power. This is what I tell pastors, ministers and evangelists. I say, get the anointing on your life. Don't try to improve your preaching, your program, your brochure, the prominence of your guest speakers or the entertainment value of your ministry to try and draw the crowds or to boost your finances. Forget about all that stuff and have an encounter with God! When the power of God is on your life, people will volunteer freely. They will say I want to serve;

I want to help; I want to give." People want to be where the power and life of God is.

The first thing the anointing does is break yokes or removes bondages and then it empowers believers for purpose and ministry. The anointing also brings favor and favor brings provision.

The book of Acts confirms this principle: And with great power the apostles gave witness to the resurrection of the Lord Jesus. And great grace was upon them all. (Acts 4:33) You see, great power brought what? Great power gave them the platform to give witness to the resurrection of the Lord Jesus and great grace or favor was upon them all. After the release of this great power in the early church, people sold their lands and houses and came and laid it at the feet of the apostles. Why? Great power brings great favor and great provision.

For those of you in ministry, the question is: What is going to set your ministry apart from all the other thousands of ministries in the kingdom today? It's not a competition we thank God for each of the ministries out there but why is anybody going to want to have you in their church? You've got to have the anointing. When you are in the anointing, just like Esther, who was prepared with oil for the king for six months and then in perfume (the presence of God), then you begin to walk in favor. The first thing the King gave her was favor.

If you don't have favor right now, you can get it by getting into the oil. When Esther soaked in oil, she found favor with the king; He gave her a place in the palace. Then the king extended his scepter and told Esther to ask whatever she wished, up to half of his kingdom. Anointed people get to ask what they wish from the King. Job also had the anointing. Let me show you why Job had the anointing:

Oh, that I were as in months past, as in the days when God watched over me; when His lamp shone upon my head, and when by His light I walked through darkness; just as I was in the days of my prime, when the friendly counsel of God was over my tent; when the Almighty was yet with me, when my children were around me; when my steps were bathed with cream, and the rock poured out rivers of oil for me! (Job 29:2-6).

Job is remembering his days of anointing when God protected him, when he walked through the darkness by God's light, the Spirit of Wisdom and Revelation.

He longed for those days when God watched over him, his house, his car, his kids, his belongings and everything that concerned him. The devil couldn't break through the supernatural hedge that was around him. Job is recalling the days of his prime when he walked in the anointing. He even speaks of the friendly inward secret of God that waited for him Job had a friendship with God. When he walked in that anointing, his children were safe from the enemy's attacks. How many of you know that when the anointing comes upon your life, it keeps your children from backsliding or draws them back to God? This is God's provision to us through the anointing. Then, in verse six, Job continues to describe the powerful anointing on his life. He says something like, Here is how anointed I was guys. I was so anointed that my steps were bathed with cream! The word cream could also be interpreted as butter. I wasn't just anointed with oil, guys. The rock gave me rivers of oil not just a touch of God's oil, but an ever-increasing, flowing river of God's oil. I was so anointed that it was as if my feet walked in butter.

Now what do buttery feet look like? In scripture, feet speak of direction? His word is a lamp to our feet. Feet also refer to your coming and going, your purpose, your life, direction and your Christian walk. When your feet walk in butter, we begin to live a smooth and peaceful gliding life it's even beyond abundance. Everything becomes easy and without effort! You don't have to bang your head up against a wall; provision and success in every area of your life just comes naturally with little effort without grueling work and without sweat. Everything just flows. God doesn't just anoint your life for supernatural ministry; he wants to put anointing on your car, your kids, your hot tub, your everyday walk, and even your dog everything! Come on. Do you have faith for these things?

When Moses anointed the tabernacle, he had to anoint the forks. Every utensil in the tabernacle had to get oil on it. Think about the anointing dripping on everything in your house. You go to pick up your coffee mug and you fall under the power. God wants to bless my stuff! Say that: God wants to bless my stuff! He wants me to live in abundance.

He certainly doesn't want us to be saying, I can't make ends meet. My needs just aren't being met. I can't get 10 people in my meetings. No. We are talking butter. Then Job continues speaking about what the anointing will do for you. When Job went out to the city he had favor with princes and Kings; he had favor with young people. And you know why he had this oil?

In chapter 29 from verse 12 on, Job describes the lifestyle that brought favor on him. He says he set the poor and the fatherless free and blessed the perishing man. Job caused the widow's heart to sing for joy. He walked in righteousness and justice. When the blind couldn't see where to go, Job became their eyes. He also became feet for the lame and helped the stranger by searching out the cases that he did not know. Job fought to set captives free, to break the fangs of the wicked and to pluck the victim from his teeth. Basically Job is saying, I cast out devils and broke demonic bondage that's why the anointing came upon my feet, my possessions and my children.

That's why I had the inward secret of God, special revelation from heaven and divine protection; that's why my life was divinely hedged about so the Devil couldn't touch me.

In the same way that God blessed Job in those days of divine oil, God also wants to bless us. God wants to pour this same anointing on our lives. But guess what? You are already delivering the poor and the victims of the enemy. You are already causing the widow's heart to sing for joy. Why? You do these things when you partner together with us. As Revival Waves of Glory goes to the poor, to the victims and to those who need to be healed and set free, you go with us. Therefore, God also wants to place this cream and butter upon your life as you partner with us or any other ministry. You need to receive this

anointing of partnership by faith. I
want to pray that the power and
favor of the anointing comes on
your life. I want to pray that God
would bring an increase of grace
and an increase of favor on your
life.

If you are interested in being a
partner with Revival Waves of Glory
please pray this prayer. If you are
not led to partner with our ministry,
don't lose this Chapter all together.
This topic of partnering with
anointed ministries works and we
have had testimonies of supporters.

Join me in this prayer:
Lord we thank you that we aren't
just partnering with a ministry really
we are partnering with you and your
gospel. Thank You that we get to
be your vessels. We are so grateful

for your many blessings upon our ministry and our lives, Father. Today, we want to seek you and we want to seek the anointing that comes from your Spirit, oh God. As Your partners, we also ask you for the revelation that comes from Your Spirit today and we want to pray that your kingdom would come today in our lives. Lord, we cry out for fresh oil from heaven. Come Holy Spirit; fill our lives with your glory, your favor and your fragrance. We receive the inheritance of partners Lord and ask for the anointing for healing, the prophetic and for mercy. God we love you today. You are so good to us.

Thank you for the opportunity to partner with you and for the many ways you have already blessed us and that you have allowed us to impact thousands throughout the nations. We thank you too, that your promise to continue to shower blessings on our lives and ministry as we do the works of Jesus for those in need. Amen.

About The Author

Bill Vincent is no stranger to understanding the power of God. Not only has he spent over twenty years as a Minister with a strong prophetic anointing, he is now also an Apostle and Author with Revival Waves of Glory Ministries in Litchfield, IL. Along with his wife, Tabitha, he, leads a team providing apostolic oversight in all aspects of ministry, including service, personal ministry and Godly character.

Bill offers a wide range of writings and teachings from deliverance, to experiencing presence of God and developing Apostolic cutting edge Church structure. Drawing on the power of the Holy Spirit through years of experience in Revival,

Spiritual Sensitivity, and deliverance ministry, Bill now focuses mainly on pursuing the Presence of God and breaking the power of the devil off of people's lives.

His books 48 and counting has since helped many people to overcome the spirits and curses of Satan. For more information or to keep up with Bill's latest releases, please visit, www.revivalwavesofgloryministries. com. To contact Bill, feel free to follow him on twitter @revivalwaves.

Recommended Products

By Bill Vincent

Overcoming Obstacles
Glory: Pursuing God's Presence
Defeating the Demonic Realm
Increasing Your Prophetic Gift
Increasing Your Anointing
Keys to Receiving Your Miracle
The Supernatural Realm
Waves of Revival
Increase of Revelation and Restoration
The Resurrection Power of God
Discerning Your Call of God
Apostolic Breakthrough
Glory: Increasing God's Presence
Love is Waiting – Don't Let Love Pass
You By
The Healing Power of God
Glory: Expanding God's Presence
Receiving Personal Prophecy
Signs and Wonders

Signs and Wonders Revelations
Children Stories
The Rapture
The Secret Place of God's Power
Building a Prototype Church
Breakthrough of Spiritual Strongholds
Glory: Revival Presence of God
Overcoming the Power of Lust
Glory: Kingdom Presence of God
Transitioning to the Prototype Church
The Stronghold of Jezebel
Healing After Divorce
A Closer Relationship With God
Cover Up and Save Yourself
Desperate for God's Presence
The War for Spiritual Battles
Spiritual Leadership
Global Warning
Millions of Churches
Destroying the Jezebel Spirit
Awakening of Miracles
Deception and Consequences Revealed
Are You a Follower of Christ

Don't Let the Enemy Steal from You!
A Godly Shaking
The Unsearchable Riches of Christ
Heaven's Court System
Satan's Open Doors
Armed for Battle
The Wrestler
Spiritual Warfare: Complete Collection
Growing In the Prophetic
The Prototype Church: Complete
Edition
Faith

To Order:
Email:
rwgcontact@yahoo.com

Web Site:
www.revivalwavesofgloryministries.
com

Mail Order:
Revival Waves of Glory
PO Box 596
Litchfield, IL 62056

Shipping $5.00
If you mail an order and pay by
check, make check out to Revival
Waves of Glory.

The Resurrection Power of God